Instructor's Manual

Composition Skills 3

The English Book

Gary W. Elliott
Jon B. Adams

SCIENCE RESEARCH ASSOCIATES, INC.
Chicago, Palo Alto, Toronto
Henley-on-Thames, Sydney, Paris

A Subsidiary of IBM

About the Authors

Gary W. Elliott is chair of the English department at Warren Junior High School, West Newton, Massachusetts. Elliott has taught English for fourteen years and has participated in workshops on English curriculum development for the city of Newton, MA. Elliott's major interest in the teaching of English is in composition.

Jon B. Adams has taught English for fourteen years and is presently a teacher of English at Warren Junior High School in West Newton, Massachusetts.

ISBN 0-574-42066-5

Reorder No. 11-3025

A RATIONALE

The design of this composition series grows out of certain basic beliefs about the student, the teacher, the writing process, the composition program, and the textbook.

First, we believe that the secondary school *student* should and can learn to write. We emphasize "student," because the series is designed to develop competent student writers, not to produce gifted professional writers. We believe that there has been too much well-intentioned but misguided analysis of how professional writers learned to write and how they compose. We do not believe that Ernest Hemingway's reflections on how he wrote a novel are always of great use to the adolescent struggling to write a paragraph. Our concern is with the student, an apprentice to the craft of writing. While we believe that any sound writing program must provide for individual differences among those students, we also are convinced that there is a common body of knowledge and repertoire of skills to be acquired.

We believe that the classroom teacher plays a central role in developing that competence in students. A responsive teacher, sensitive to individual needs and aware of unique problems, is essential in creating an environment for writing, stimulating the writing process, and facilitating the acquisition of those skills. It is thus patently absurd to attempt to develop a "teacher-proof" curriculum or publish "teacher-proof" materials. The goal, instead, is to develop materials that will support, not control or obstruct, the teacher-student interaction.

The special focus of these interactions, of course, is on the writing process and its product. While we know both from direct experience and the testimony of others that the process varies with the writer and the work, we believe that the findings of such investigators as Janet Emig (1971) and James Britton (1975) do help us understand which processes seem most productive for the apprentice writer. The stages identified by Britton—*conception, incubation, production,* and *revision*—seem especially useful in planning and developing instructional materials. And it seems to us that the prewriting activities of the conception and incubation stages deserve special emphasis in a work of this sort. Here the findings of Josephine Miles (1963) relative to the importance of predication seem especially relevant, and we are happy to acknowledge our indebtedness to her work.

The specific ways in which these processes result in a finished piece of writing depend greatly, of course, upon the purpose of the writing. We concur here with Kinneavy's (1971) observation that "purpose in discourse is all important. The aim of discourse determines everything else in the process of discourse" (p. 48). And aim, of course, is closely linked to the mode of discourse, four of which are identified by Kinneavy: *expressive, literary, persuasive,* and *referential.* The aim of expressive discourse is simply to express the writer's personality or point of view. The purpose of literary discourse is to create a literary artifact "worthy of appreciation in its own right" (p. 39). Persuasive discourse attempts to bring about a change in an audience's point of view or to influence an audience to take an action. And referential discourse tries only to designate or reproduce reality. The reader here will note some similarity between the four modes delineated by Kinneavy and the three used by Britton. Britton found three modes most useful in guiding his own research: the *expressive* (similar to Kinneavy's); the *transactional* (subsuming Kinneavy's "persuasive" and "referential"), and the *poetic* (similar to Kinneavy's "literary"). Both Britton and Kinneavy stress the importance of providing instruction and practice in all modes, a point of view with which we strongly concur.

What type of curriculum design and instructional practice will help the student communicate effectively in all modes? In answering this question, we have found it most helpful to posit three degrees of structure in the writing program: *open structure, moderate structure,* and *high structure.* The terms are best understood in reference to this matrix, which analyzes structure in terms of two components—the aspect of writing and the locus of the decision.

In a writing assignment (or program) with open structure, all deci-

Aspect of Writing	LOCUS OF DECISION		
	Open Structure	*Moderate Structure*	*High Structure*
1. Topic or subject	self	self or other	other
2. Mode of discourse	self	self or other	other
3. Purpose	self	self or other	other
4. Audience	self	self or other	other
5. Methods used	self	self or other	other
6. Style of writing	self	self or other	other
7. Length of product	self	self or other	other
8. Time and deadline	self	self or other	other
9. Source and type of evaluation	self	self or other	other

sions are made by the writer; in an assignment (or program) with high structure, the decisions are made by someone else (a teacher, a text, an editor, a supervisor). In an assignment (or program) with moderate structure, some of these decisions are made by the self and some by another.

The best writer, we believe, is one who can write effectively with all types of structure—who can write with complete autonomy but who can also produce effective writing when someone else has set the specifications. Those who argue for a completely open writing program forget that much adult writing is produced under conditions of high structure. The student who has been told only, "Write what you wish when you are inspired" later has trouble with a teacher or supervisor who says, "I need this report by tomorrow." These arguments suggest, therefore, that a comprehensive writing program will provide for all three degrees of structure and that a wise teacher will systematically vary the aspects of structure.

We also believe that such a comprehensive writing program should include all the modes of discourse, providing systematic instruction and practice in those modes through a developmental sequence of units covering the six years of secondary education. We concur with Moffett (1968) that the expressive mode should receive major emphasis in the elementary school, most often in conditions of open structure; but we also believe that the secondary school student can profit from a program that gives close attention to the other modes as well, sometimes in conditions of high structure. In fact, one could argue that, while the student should have much opportunity to use the expressive mode, the instructional program should give primary emphasis to the persuasive and referential, since these two modes play the most important roles in school, college, and life and are those where deficiencies are most apparent.

A sound textbook series will play an important part in such a program, especially in the structured aspects of the curriculum. There is little need for a textbook to attempt to structure what should remain open. It is here that the teacher plays a crucial role, both in knowing when to provide conditions of open structure and in knowing how to use the text to provide the degree and type of structure needed. The most successful text, therefore, is one that is most teachable—that does the best possible job of providing the necessary structure for the teacher to use flexibly and imaginatively.

AN OVERVIEW

The beliefs articulated above have informed the design and development of this comprehensive series of composition texts, which we hope will assist school districts and classroom teachers in improving the writing of all students. The program has four major components: *the writing process, the elements of composition, the modes of discourse,* and *the revising process*. Both the second and third of these components are further subdivided, yielding eleven separate yet related strands, as follows:

The Writing Process
The Elements of Composition
    Words
    Sentences
    Paragraphs
The Modes of Discourse
    Personal Writing
    Writing about Literature
    Exposition
    Argumentation
    Applied Writing Skills
    Writing Across the Curriculum
The Revising Process

As the sequence chart on pages 6 and 7 indicates, these eleven strands are carefully developed through six levels, in general corresponding to the six grades of secondary school. Each level builds upon preceding levels in a developmental sequence; yet there is sufficient review so that each book stands on its own. The chart notes the primary emphasis of the new material introduced but for the most part does not reflect the systematic review built into each book. The order in which the strands are listed in the chart is the order in which they appear in the texts; and, in general, one chapter is devoted to each strand. Each book concludes with a "Writer's Handbook," a compendium of definitions and suggestions.

Each book begins with an examination of the process of writing. As noted above, this strand draws from the work of Josephine Miles in stressing the importance of predication in the composing process.

The "composing process" chapters also incorporate James Moffett's (1968) ideas about speaker/audience and speaker/subject relationships and encourage the students, in line with Moffett's own suggestions, to talk and discuss in order to generate ideas for writing. These chapters give students the greatest opportunity to write in the expressive mode, and each chapter in this strand encourages the student to transform expressive beginnings into a more finished literary form.

The next three chapters in each book deal systematically with the elements of composition. First, a chapter on word choice helps the student choose the correct word and the effective word. The "correct word" section in each book contains a basic list of words frequently confused and misused. The "effective word" section treats progressively and developmentally such concerns as connotation and denotation, abstract and concrete words, sensory images, jargon and euphemisms, words and audiences. These matters are not presented in isolation but are dealt with in the context of writing with a definite purpose for a specified audience.

The "sentence" strand accomplishes several important objectives. The first is to give the student a basic knowledge of sentence parts and sentence patterns, so as to establish a knowledge of this fundamental content and to provide student and teacher with a common vocabulary for examining the written sentence. The second objective is to give the student instruction and directed practice in learning how to fashion more effective sentences, using the processes developed by Francis Christensen (1968). The third objective is to help the student develop a more mature style through the use of both open and controlled sentence combining strategies. The research of Mellon (1969), O'Hare (1971), and others, we believe, is persuasive in its conclusion that such sentence combining practice will produce a more mature sentence style. Finally, the "sentence" chapters help the student evaluate his or her own sentences and master the skills needed for improving incorrect and ineffective sentences.

The "paragraph" strand offers the student specific and systematic help in organizing and developing several types of paragraphs. While the emphasis is on the careful crafting of the paragraph, the student learns that the paragraph is only one part of a longer essay and that the shape and form of the paragraph are directly influenced by decisions made about the essay. Here again the paragraph chapter makes explicit reference to the contributions of Christensen, but the books do not limit themselves to his theories. Instead the books build upon Christensen's ideas by showing how other types of paragraph plans and patterns can be used to communicate a message. The chapters on the paragraph are honest about such matters as the topic sentence and methods of development in a way in which other texts unfortunately have not been: the point is made that the topic sentence and the several types of development are useful pedagogical devices for the beginning writer to master— but they are not always used by professional writers. We think Braddock's observation is most appropriate here:

> Teachers and textbook writers should exercise caution in making statements about the frequency with which contemporary professional writers use simple or even explicit topic sentences in expository paragraphs. It is abundantly clear that students should not be told that professional writers usually begin their paragraphs with topic sentences. . . . While helping students use clear topic sentences in their writing and identify variously presented topical ideas in their reading, the teacher should not pretend that professional writers largely follow the practices he is advocating (1974, p. 302).

Our own division of the modes of discourse reflects the reality of the secondary school classroom and the world of work rather than the theory of rhetoricians. The strand begins with "personal writing," that which is closest and perhaps most important to the student. The "personal writing" strand is, obviously, very much concerned with the type of writing which both Britton and Kinneavy call "expressive": the writing that derives primarily from the student's own experience and is chiefly con-

Strand/Level	1	2	3
			THE SKILLS OF COMPOSING:
The Process of Writing	Steps in the Writing Process	Observing and Selecting for Purpose	Prewriting, Composing, and Editing
The Word	Effective and Correct Words	Appropriateness and Clarity	Connotation, Denotation; Abstract and Concrete Words
The Sentence	Sentence Parts and Patterns; Combining Basic Patterns	Developing the Basic Patterns; Combining with Grammatical Structures	Clarity, Economy, and Variety in Sentence Use; Sentence Combining
The Paragraph	The Nature of the Paragraph	Types of Paragraphs and Their Development	Writing Paragraphs from Personal and Print Sources
Personal Writing	Creating a Story	Observing Your World	Using Your Experiences
Writing About Literature	Responding to Literature	Writing the Library Paper	Reviewing Nonfiction
Argumentation	Expressing an Opinion	Defending an Opinion	Using Persuasion
Exposition	Giving Directions; Explaining a Process	Explaining Your World	Writing a Causal Analysis
Applied Writing Skills	The Friendly Letter; The Business Letter	Letters of Criticism and Appreciation; The Social Note; Order Forms	Letters for Career Information; Letters to Public Officials; The Note of Appreciation
Writing Across the Curriculum	School Paragraphs	School Essays	Library Paper; Essay Tests
The Revising Process	How to Revise	Steps in the Revising Process	Improving through Revision
Writer's Handbook A glossary of grammar and composition terms, including			

cerned with articulating personal feelings and experiences. Successive books try to move the student from a concern about self to a concern about others and then to the larger world. And in every case the chapter suggests ways by which the student can transform expressive beginnings into literary forms.

A separate strand on "writing about literature" is included because we believe that such writing often involves the expressive, transactional, and poetic modes in a way challenging to the student—and is also important in and of itself. In this strand we have drawn from the findings of Purves and Beach (1972) in developing our own model of the reading-responding interaction:

A DEVELOPMENTAL SEQUENCE

4 Predication and Representation	5 Distance and Focus	6 Voice, Symbol, and Form
Guidelines for Effective Word Choice	Words for School and Career	Words and the Writer's Purpose
Sentence Combining; Improved Sentences	Writing Effective Sentences through Combining Strategies	Developing a Mature Sentence Style
Paragraph Patterns	Solving Paragraph Problems	The Rhetoric of the Paragraph
Creating a Biography	Picturing People and Places	Explaining a World
Writing about Novels	Writing the Research Paper	Responding to Poetry
Writing Effective Persuasive Essays	Writing Argumentation	Developing Effective Arguments
Writing the Essay of Classification	Making Comparisons and Contrasts	Combining Expository Types and Skills
Letters of Application; The Job Application; Invitations	Letters for College and Career; The College Application; Writing the Career Paper	Technical Writing; The Resumé; The Letter of Application; Formal Invitations
Reporting on Investigations; Essay Answers	Biographical Research; Essay Answers	Teacher Questions
Revising and Rewriting	Using Peer Review and Teacher Evaluation	Stages in the Revision Process
usage notes and suggestions for writing		

You read to . . .	And when you respond, you . . .
comprehend the surface ⟶	describe the surface meaning of the work
identify with the work ⟶	respond personally to the work
understand the deeper ⟶ meaning of the work	interpret the deeper meaning of the work
judge the value of the work →	evaluate the achievement of the work

The chapters help the student use the model to respond to nonfiction, novels, and poetry; in addition, the strand includes chapters on writing a reference or research paper about a problem related to language or literature.

The several chapters on exposition are concerned exclusively with what Kinneavy calls "referential" writing—writing that explains the world out there. In this strand the levels focus on skills of increasing complexity, beginning with the simple process of giving directions and concluding with ways to combine several expository processes in one longer essay. The essays of causal analysis, classification, and comparison-contrast are treated separately; in every case, however, the expository essays draw from the student's internalized or acquired knowledge. In this way the student is helped to understand that even referential writing is personal, requiring a commitment of the self. All the exposition chapters stress the importance of adaptation to audience.

Although the terms *essay of opinion, persuasion,* and *argumentation* are often used interchangeably in other texts, we have tried in this series to differentiate them for the purposes of this strand: *opinion* is the simplest, the mere expression of a belief with an explanation of the reasons for that belief; *persuasion* is an attempt to move an audience by a variety of emotional and rational appeals; and *argumentation*, intellectually the most rigorous, uses sound reasoning to advance and rebut arguments. The chapters in this strand give special attention to both audience and medium, since these two aspects of the communication context are most important in shaping such messages.

The next mode we call "applied writing skills," which includes the practical writing used in life outside the school. Three general types of writing are emphasized here: the letters and notes needed for personal and social occasions; the letters and forms required in the worlds of work and higher education; and the writing used as a citizen and as a consumer. In each case these several forms are presented in a sequence based upon the developing needs and interests of the adolescent. The emphasis is on practical writing the student can use now—not writing to be used in some remote adult period of life.

The final mode, "writing across the curriculum," reflects the current concern in both this country and England to help students acquire the skills needed to write clear and effective academic discourse, both in English classes and in other school subjects. Since academic discourse plays a less important role in the early years of junior high school, the skills required are not treated in a separate chapter in the first two books but instead are integrated throughout the text. In the last four books, however, explicit and separate attention is given to such skills as reporting on investigations, answering essay questions, writing biographical research, and responding to teacher questions.

Although revision is only one step in the writing process, we believe it is important enough to warrant separate treatment. These chapters give the student specific techniques for improving a paper before it is submitted, for evaluating one's own work and the work of peers, and for revising a paper after it has been graded.

And, as noted above, each book concludes with a "Writer's Handbook," a glossary of terms used in grammar and composition. Each term is defined simply and clearly and is illustrated with examples, where appropriate. Practical suggestions for writing are offered as they relate to a given term. Each handbook includes all the terms used in previous books as well as the new terms introduced in that particular text.

We believe that the series as designed offers a complete writing program for the structured part of the English composition curriculum. The effective teacher will, of course, supplement the text with additional assignments and will provide many other opportunities for the extemporaneous writing that flows immediately from the student's inner world. We feel confident that these texts in the hands of such a teacher will result in a highly successful composition program.

USING THE TEXT IN A COMPREHENSIVE WRITING PROGRAM

As should be obvious from the beliefs stated above, we strongly encourage teachers to use the books as flexibly and imaginatively as they can. Some guidelines for effective use, however, can be suggested, based upon Britton's insightful analysis of the composing process of student writers. As noted above, Britton identifies four stages in this process: *conception, incubation, production,* and *revision.* His insights about each of these stages suggest some guidelines for effective pedagogical practice.

Conception: The writer decides to write. Some specific incident (perhaps purely mental) provokes this decision to write. Most often in school writing, the teacher's assignment is the inciting incident. For some students, specific demands in the assignment seem to facilitate; for others, they obstruct. But based upon either internal decisions or external demands, the writer searches and explores his or her experience. The conception stage may be short or long. It is completed when the writer knows what he or she is going to write and has formed some sense of what is expected.

Incubation: Once the idea is conceived, the writer then needs time for incubation to reflect, plan, check the facts, and, as Britton says, "get it right with the self." Thus, an activity important in the incubation stage is explaining to oneself—talking things over in a dialog with the self. At this stage, as Lundsteen (1976) notes, good talk with others is also very helpful, for such open discussion gives the writer a chance to express tentative conclusions, try out ideas, and hear other points of view. When the task is simple and the message is clearly known, the incubation stage can be short. Complex writing tasks or dimly perceived understandings require more time for incubation.

Production: With these two prewriting stages completed, the student writer begins to produce or articulate. It is a period of intense concentration when interruptions are not welcomed and when direct advice from the teacher often seems resented. If the production is done in the classroom, the teacher can easily observe the characteristic behaviors of the writer at work: deep concentration, bursts of writing with many pauses, much scanning of what has been written. Here the reflective writer learns first-hand why writing has so often been described as a process of discovery. The struggle to articulate becomes the way of discerning.

Revision: The revision stage is not simply a time of catching errors; it is also a time for re-visioning, for rethinking what one has said — and then determining if it has been said in the best way possible.

These stages are not always discrete, of course; often they run together in ways difficult to separate. Yet their delineation does help us understand how we can manage things instructionally in order to get the best results.

Knowing then what we do about these stages, what use of the text and which teaching practice will produce these results? The answers will, of course, vary with the student, the teacher, and the type of writing. However, some answers can be offered if we consider how a typical assignment and chapter might be handled for an average tenth-grade student. As the chart on page 12 indicates, we see the student, the teacher, and the text working together and interactively throughout the four stages over a period of time. While the time will vary with the student and the way the teacher manages the composition class, a period of five days will often be required for the entire process. Not all of this will be class time, obviously, and in some cases the stages will be telescoped. However, the need to provide adequate time for all four stages and to offer specific instruction where it is most needed suggests that better results will probably be obtained if a smaller number of themes are assigned and taught carefully. Here we concur with the observation of Elizabeth F. Haynes, who, after reviewing all the pertinent research, made this recommendation:

> Teachers should give greater emphasis to the guiding of careful development of a limited number of papers, with attention given to direct methods of instruction and to the solving of communication problems before and during the writing process, rather than on the hurried production of a great number of papers (1978, p. 87).

The same recommendation was made strongly by Charles Stallard (1974) after he analyzed the writing and composing process of fifteen "good" student writers. In comparison with a group of fifteen randomly selected students, the good writers spent more time contemplating, planning writing, and revising.

This conclusion and the testimony of other successful teachers support the need for the kind of direct instruction suggested in the chart. Although there is always an imperative need to individualize instruction in such matters, it is apparent that certain writing skills are important throughout the four stages. And these skills will be most efficiently and effectively taught, we believe, by text and teacher working together.

The text, then, has been designed with this use in mind—to be an effective tool in the hands of a skilled teacher, who is teaching specific writing skills through the medium of carefully planned assignments.

Teachers will vary, of course, in the order in which they present the chapters and teach the related skills. Some will find it simpler to use the sequence of the chapters as the basic organizational plan for the year's work, with only slight modification, thus:

1. The Process of Writing	Teach content in "The
2. The Word	Revising Process" and
3. The Sentence	"A Writer's Handbook"
4. The Paragraph	as needed
5. Personal Writing	
6. Writing about Literature	
7. Exposition	
8. Argumentation	
9. Applied Writing Skills	
10. Writing Across the Curriculum	

Other teachers with less motivated students, perhaps, will wish to begin the year by emphasizing the expressive writing found in the chapters on "process" and "personal writing," using the chapters on word, sentence, and paragraph to break up the emphasis on transactional writing. Their plan might look like this:

1. The Process of Writing	Teach content in "The
2. Personal Writing	Revising Process" and
3. The Word	"A Writer's Handbook"
4. Writing about Literature	as needed
5. The Sentence	
6. Exposition	
7. The Paragraph	
8. Argumentation	
9. Applied Writing Skills	
10. Writing Across the Curriculum	

Another plan would emphasize the incremental development:

1. The Word	Use content in "A
2. The Sentence	Writer's Handbook" as
3. The Paragraph	needed
4. The Writing Process	
5. The Revising Process	
6. Personal Writing	
7. Writing about Literature	
8. Exposition	
9. Argumentation	
10. Applied Writing Skills	
11. Writing Across the Curriculum	

The point, obviously, is that the books have been designed to be used flexibly. Chapters build upon and refer to each other, but each stands on its own and does not require mastery of some preceding chapter.

FACILITATING THE WRITING PROCESSES

Stage	Student	Teacher	Text	Time
Conception	Reflects on experience; Exchanges ideas about topic possibilities; Selects topic	Provides supportive environment; Discusses topic possibilities; Stimulates writing; Determines optimal structure needed	Suggests topics; Explains and illustrates invention process	1 day
Incubation	Explains to self; Talks out ideas; Selects and uses best planning model; Assembles needed information	Provides opportunity for and encourages open discussion; Helps student select best planning model; Makes resources available; Recognizes need for and provides time for incubation	Explains planning process; Suggests ways of getting started; Suggests ways of locating materials	1-2 days
Production	Tries exercises; Explores ideas and rethinks topic; Applies methods to help in production-articulation; Shapes preliminary draft	Offers individual help when asked without interruptions; Adds own ideas about methods; Explains, clarifies methods; Selects most useful exercises; Provides atmosphere conducive to production when writing is done in class	Explains useful methods; Offers models; Provides for guided practice	2-3 days
Revision	Reviews, rethinks ideas; Evaluates writing; Revises	Offers individual help as needed; Explains, clarifies revising process	Explains revision process; Suggests criteria for evaluation; Provides resources for checking writing	1 day

It has also been our intent in designing and writing these books to provide some useful answers to the questions most frequently asked by conscientious teachers of writing:

1. *"How can I help my students get ideas?"* Every chapter, where appropriate, gives the student very specific suggestions about topics—and, more important, about processes to use to generate ideas. The teacher is encouraged to spend sufficient class time early in the year to discuss these processes and to use them together with the students, so that the students see first-hand how certain analytical processes can yield fruitful results. Most chapters also culminate in an "Application," a major writing task that requires the student to synthesize what has been learned. In addition, where the teacher feels the student needs an even more definitive structure, carefully worked assignments have been provided. The assignments vary intentionally in their degree of openness and require the student to write in a variety of modes for different audiences, with different purposes.

2. *"How can I help my students plan their writing more carefully?"* The books make this basic point at every appropriate juncture: good writing is writing which has been carefully planned. Sometimes the planning is only mental, and the best plans often emerge organically as the writing progresses—but there is no substitute for planning. A variety of planning models is presented, including the standard outline, and sample plans are offered for analysis. We would hope that the teacher would help the student discover, perhaps by trial and error, which planning process for that individual results in the best writing. A good outline, in our view, is only a means to an end.

3. *"How can I teach the specific skills the students need for a given assignment?"* One of the strengths of the books, we believe, is that each chapter identifies the specific skills needed to accomplish a writing task, explains those skills in terms the students can understand, shows those skills at work in professional writing, and presents a variety of exercises requiring the application of those skills. For most students, we believe, such a step-by-step process will provide the structure they need to produce well-crafted prose. And we would encourage the teacher, especially in the first few months of the academic year, to devote sufficient class time to a careful analysis and explanation of these materials. There will, of course, be very able students impatient with such a step-by-step approach—and teachers who do not see the need for detailed analysis in the classroom. In such situations the teacher can assign these sections for study outside the class, holding the student responsible only for demonstrating those skills in the final product.

4. *"How can I help my students revise and evaluate their own work?"* In addition to the separate chapter on revision, which is probably best used early in the year, each relevant chapter makes specific suggestions about revising and improving writing. And most of the chapters which deal with the longer essay conclude with specific criteria which the student can use in a self-evaluation.

For major writing assignments, teachers are encouraged to discuss those criteria with the students, show the students how those criteria can be applied to student writing, and give the students class time to evaluate their own and their classmates' papers.

5. *"How can I help less able students develop writing skills?"* One of the strengths of the text, we believe, is that its clear, step-by-step approach takes the mystery out of writing; it should therefore prove helpful to students who have problems at all stages of the writing process. However, the least verbal students may need some special assistance like the following:

   a. *Let them talk first, then write.* Show them how to talk out their ideas to a peer, to you, or to a tape recorder, and then write what they have spoken.

   b. *Provide a supportive atmosphere which encourages all writing efforts.* Such students need some negative feedback when that is appropriate, but they have experienced so much failure with writing that they can use more praise and encouragement at the outset. Set realistic standards for them—but do not accept careless or half-hearted attempts.

   c. *Legitimate giving and receiving help.* Peer tutoring can improve writing, but you must take special pains to be sure that the tutor does not do the actual writing. Take time to train tutors so that they know what kind of help is acceptable—and what kind is dishonest.

   d. *Give special attention to the whole theme.* We think teachers who emphasize only sentences and paragraphs with less able students are misguided. Even such students need to understand that most writing does not take the form of a single paragraph. It is our experience that these students can learn to write longer papers, given enough help. And in teaching and grading such longer papers, emphasize (at least at the outset) such matters as the quality of ideas and organization, rather than focusing on spelling, sentence structure, and punctuation.

   e. *Create real audiences and writing needs for these students.* The less able student especially needs to feel that he or she is writing for a real purpose and a real audience. Class magazines and peer reading sessions therefore become especially important.

REFERENCES

Braddock, R. "The Frequency and Placement of Topic Sentences in Expository Prose," *Research in the Teaching of English*, 1974, 8, 287-302.

Britton, J. and others. *The Development of Writing Abilities* (11-18). London: Macmillan Education, 1975.

Christensen, F. *Notes Toward a New Rhetoric.* New York: Harper and Row, 1968.

Emig, J. *The Composing Process of Twelfth Graders* (NCTE Research Report No. 13). Urbana, IL: National Council of Teachers of English, 1971.

Haynes, E. "Using Research in Preparing to Teach Writing," *English Journal*, 1978, 1, 82-88.

Kinneavy, J. *A Theory of Discourse.* Englewood Cliffs, NJ: Prentice Hall, 1971.

Lundsteen, S., ed. *Help for the Teacher of Written Composition*. Urbana, IL: National Conference on Research in English, 1976.

Mellon, J. *Transformational Sentence Combining*. Urbana, IL: National Council of Teachers of English, 1969.

Miles, J. *What We Compose*. Urbana, IL: National Council of Teachers of English, 1963.

Moffett, J. *Teaching the University of Discourse*. New York: Houghton Mifflin, 1968.

O'Hare, F. *Sentence-Combining: Improving Student Writing Without Formal Grammar Instruction*. Urbana, IL: National Council of Teachers of English, 1973.

Purves, A. and R. Beach. *Literature and the Reader: Research in Response to Literature, Reading Interests, and the Teaching of Literature*. Urbana, IL: National Council of Teachers of English, 1972.

Stallard, C. "An Analysis of the Writing Behavior of Good Student Writers," *Research in the Teaching of English*, 1974, 8, 206-218.

PROFESSIONAL RESOURCES IN THE TEACHING OF COMPOSITION

Blount, N. "Research on Teaching Literature, Language, and Composition," *Second Handbook of Research on Teaching*, edited by M. Travers. Chicago: Rand McNally, 1973.

Braddock, R., R. Lloyd-Jones, and L. Schoer. *Research in Written Composition*. Urbana, IL: National Council of Teachers of English, 1963.

Cazden, C. *Child Language and Education*. New York: Holt, Rinehart and Winston, 1972.

Clapp, O., ed. *On Righting Writing: Classroom Practices in Teaching English, 1975-76*. Urbana, IL: National Council of Teachers of English, 1975.

Cooper, C. and L. Odell. *Evaluating Writing*. Urbana, IL: National Council of Teachers of English, 1977.

Elbow, P. *Writing Without Teachers*. New York: Oxford University Press, 1973.

Gibson, W. *Persona: A Style Study for Readers and Writers*. New York: Random House, 1969.

Hawkins, T. *Group Inquiry Techniques for Teaching Writing*. Urbana, IL: National Council of Teachers of English, 1976.

Hunt, K. *Grammatical Structures Written at Three Grade Levels*. Urbana, IL: National Council of Teachers of English, 1965.

Kinneavy, J. *A Theory of Discourse*. Englewood Cliffs, NJ: Prentice Hall, 1971.

Lundsteen, S. *Help for the Teacher of Written Composition*. Urbana, IL: National Conference on Research in English, 1976.

Martin, N. and others. *Writing and Language Across the Curriculum, 11-16*. London: Ward Lock Educational, 1976.

Mellon, J. *National Assessment and the Teaching of English*. Urbana, IL: National Council of Teachers of English, 1975.

Moffett, J. *Teaching the Universe of Discourse*. New York: Houghton Mifflin, 1968.

O'Hare, F. *Sentence-Combining: Improving Student Writing Without Formal Grammar Instruction*. Urbana, IL: National Council of Teachers of English, 1973.

Shaughnessy, M. *Errors and Expectations: A Guide for the Teacher of Basic Writing*. New York: Oxford University Press, 1977.

Tate, G. *Teaching Composition: 10 Bibliographical Essays*. Fort Worth, TX: Texas Christian University Press, 1976.

Young, R., A. Becker, and K. Pike. *Rhetoric: Discovery and Change*. New York: Harcourt Brace World, 1970.

SUGGESTIONS FOR USING INDIVIDUAL CHAPTERS

Chapter 1: The Writing Process

An Overview of the Chapter

Chapter 1 introduces a broad and comprehensive view of the writing process. *Prewriting, observing, organizing,* and *revising* are identified and explained as the four basic components of the process. Specific exercises in each of these areas are presented to help students understand the unique importance of these elements to the writing process. This comprehensive view of writing is extremely helpful to the many students who think of writing in bits and pieces rather than as a unified process.

The writing suggestions help students discover topics for writing. Ideas for finding out "what you have to say" through listing, using verbs, using pictures, and using the literature of others are discussed.

Observing exercises encourage students to use sensory detail to create vivid sentences, to distinguish between fact and opinion, to recognize the importance of distance, and to understand and consider point of view.

The organizing section teaches organization through the use of metaphor, rhythm, audience consideration, form change, and paragraphing.

Finally, in "Revising, Reviewing, and Editing" students learn that the process of editing involves "looking at and changing writing to make it better." In this section exercises are provided to test students' ability to reorganize the writing of others.

Suggestions for Using the Chapter

Since this chapter introduces a general and comprehensive view of the writing process, it will be profitable to complete it first. Students will then have a frame of reference for what the text refers to as the process of writing. This frame will help students immediately to recognize the essential characteristics of the writer's task.

An understanding of prewriting, observing, organizing, and revising will give students a specific and concrete idea of those ingredients underlying successful writing.

These additional suggestions may be used to expand, develop, and reinforce the ideas introduced in the text.

Prewriting

1. *Memory Writing*: Ask students to list at least ten events that they recall from their childhood. Students should omit any events which have occurred during the last three years. Have students select one of the events listed and expand it into one or several paragraphs which include every detail they recall about the event. Then have students rewrite the paper including imaginary or con-

trived details which give a more complete and more interesting content.

2. *Writing Thoughts*: Ask students to write exactly, word for word, the actual thoughts that are running through their minds. Ask them to continue this writing for at least five minutes of class time. These thoughts could be written in a journal at the beginning of each class period for several weeks after which time students could record them for quality of ideas and sources of writing topics for longer stories or essays. Students who are willing might share their "journal" writing with the class for discussion.

3. *Using Music*: Using music to stimulate writing is often effective. Play any classical music selection for ten minutes, having students write spontaneously while listening to the music. From these writings, topics for more structured and focused writing might be selected. Have several students read what they have written. Then discuss with the class possible topics for longer essays which are apparent in the spontaneous writings.

4. *Using Imagination and Projection*: Ask students to imagine themselves to be a teacher in the school, the school principal, their mother or father, the local chief of police, or captain of the local fire department. Once they have chosen a specific person whose identity they will assume, have them write one or several paragraphs explaining, from the point of view of their assumed character, the most exciting part of their job, the most interesting aspect of their life, or the most frustrating problems they face every day.

5. *Using News Stories*: Ask students to read through the major stories of their local newspaper. Have them select one story which has aroused some feelings in them. Ask the students to write one or several paragraphs explaining those feelings.

Observing

1. *The School Yard*: On a given day ask students to observe a single location at three different time periods. For example, students might observe the school yard in the morning before classes have begun, at noon during the lunch break, and in the afternoon when classes have ended. Ask students to list details in the scene during each time period and then write a separate paragraph describing the location at each time.

2. *A Bus Ride*: Ask students to take a bus or other mass transit ride with a class member. On the ride each student should list in a notebook all observable details which strike them as interesting or unique including colors, shapes, textures, interesting people and objects. In class students might compare their lists and discuss differences in their observations.

3. *A Public Place (Zoo; Museum; Ice Capades; Basketball, Hockey or Baseball Game; Public Protest)*: Have students write one or several paragraphs explaining the feelings of an animal or object in a public place; for example, a lion in a zoo, a famous painting in a museum, a hockey puck or basketball in a game, a poster or placard at a public protest.

4. *A Television Show*: Have students choose a television show to

watch. Ask students to write one paragraph explaining why the show is unique and exciting and one paragraph explaining why the show is ordinary and dull.

Organizing

1. Ask students to write a few sentences explaining the most interesting, most frustrating, or most boring part of their day to each of the following audiences. The event explained must remain the same for each audience.
   a. a younger brother or sister
   b. a girlfriend or boyfriend
   c. the school principal
   d. a teacher
   e. a mother or father
   f. a particular friend that needs to be impressed
2. If possible, borrow or rent the film "An Occurrence at Owl Creek Bridge." Before having students view the film, have them read the Ambrose Bierce story of the same title on which the film is based. When students have finished both, ask them to write one or several paragraphs explaining the difference in organization between the film and the story. (This exercise will work with any story you can present to the students in more than one form.)
3. Ask students to discuss organizational differences between a photo-essay of their school and a written essay about their school.
   a. Where might the photo-essay begin?
   b. Where or how might the written essay begin?
   c. What photographs would make up the main body of the photo-essay?
   d. What ideas would become topics of the main paragraphs of the written essay?
   e. How would the photo-essay conclude?
   f. How would the written essay conclude?
   g. Could both have the same impact? Explain.

Editing

Since editing involves the rearrangement of written ideas so that those ideas are presented more correctly, clearly, appropriately, and effectively, students should be encouraged to edit their own work carefully. As part of composition assignments, ask students to choose, or assign to students, an editing or proofreading partner. These partners could then, for one or several composition assignments, work closely with each other during the final stages of writing, the reviewing, revising, proofreading, and editing of papers.

Chapter 2: Words

An Overview of the Chapter

The chapter is concerned with the important decisions writers must make when choosing words. In a simple way successful writing may be viewed as a process of selecting and arranging words to produce effective and clear written expressions. The chapter makes the point that good writing is rooted in careful word choice. Decisions about the use and misuse of repetition, the use of highly connotative or neutral words, the use of abstract or concrete words, and the use of specific or general words are carefully explained and studied through many related exercises. Sensory words and figurative language are also stressed and exercises on hyperbole, metaphor, personification, and simile are provided. The inappropriate use of slang, jargon, colloquialism, and cliché is explained. The chapter concludes with exercises in the proper use of thirty most confused and misused words. A list of these words with their definitions and an explanation of proper use is provided.

Suggestions for Using the Chapter

Although the skills discussed here can be continually used whenever any proofreading is requested or desired, it could be useful and rewarding to stress the skills of word choice and usage as a separate and valuable skill that relates to all communication in writing or speech. A very realistic approach to this chapter is one that stresses personal communication success as well as success in composing required writing assignments. Some suggested activities that can be used follow.

1. Lead the class in a full discussion and listing of slang and colloquial expressions present in their vocabulary. This discussion can be highlighted by stressing the denotative meanings of many of the colloquial and slang expressions, causing the expression to become ludicrous and in many cases, meaningless. The discussion should sharpen student awareness of word choice.
2. This activity has proven to be very useful in helping students discover the power of the metaphor and the simile. Follow these directions in order:
   a. With the entire class make a chalkboard list of at least twenty-five famous people with whom every member of the class is familiar. This list could easily be made by placing categories on the board, such as musical personalities, political personalities, film personalities, etc.
   b. The class may work from the list on the board or the list of famous personalities may be typed on a ditto and used in class the next day.
   c. Each student is to choose one of the famous personalities without telling any of the others in class (including the teacher).
   d. Using a piece of notebook paper or index cards, each student is to develop answers to the following for the famous personality he or she has chosen. In order for the game to be successful, it is important that nothing be *directly* indicated about the person chosen. Such things as age, race, sex, occupation, hobbies, and social status should not be directly indicated as these would tend to give away the identity of the person. The following statements are to be completed on the notebook paper or the index card.

If the person were a piece of furniture, the person would be _____.

Example: An enormous old, richly-decorated, living-room chair with soft cushioned arms and an extremely comfortable seat.

If the person were an automobile, the person would be _____.
If the person were an animal, the person would be _____.
If the person were a type of tree or flower, the person would be _____.
If the person were a certain color, the person would be _____.
If the person were a piece of clothing, the person would be _____.
If the person were a specific type of day, the person would be _____.
If the person were a specific room in my house, the person would be _____.

Original categories for metaphor-making, such as type of machinery, piece of jewelry, piece of silverware, may be presented by each student.
  e. Students should then take their list of metaphors and individually read them to the class, allowing the class to ask additional questions, if necessary.
  f. Students in class should attempt to identify from their list the famous person referred to in the metaphors presented.
  g. Follow up with a discussion of the significance of image and metaphor.
3. Have each student write a poetic prose paragraph describing a person (perhaps a fellow classmate) but not mentioning the person's name in the description. Pronouns of identification may be used in the paragraph. The paragraph should be read to the class, and the class should attempt to identify the person. The purpose of this activity, however, is in the quality of the poetic writing, not in the guessing.
4. Creating Japanese Haiku poetry is often useful when discussing figures of speech and the value of words. The rules for writing Haiku should be explained and strictly followed. It is a poem of three lines with each line having a specific number of syllables as follows: five in the first, seven in the second, five in the third. The poem must contain one or more figures of speech and must refer to both time and nature. No line should rhyme and no line should end with a conjunction. To write a quality Haiku is challenging, in that a true Japanese Haiku creates a profound thought about life through its gentle poetic imagery.
5. Have the students construct generalization columns. A generalization column is a list of words that builds from a specific word to a general term or the reverse.

Examples:

living thing	piece of metal
animal	utensil
canine	eating tool
pet	silverware
dog	spoon
Duke	soup spoon

6. Discuss with the class these faulty expressions often found in their speech and, consequently, put into their writing.
  a. can, may
  b. really good, really bad

c. guess, think
d. just
e. and etc.
f. at about, around about
g. funny, strange, tragic
h. lot, lots of, many, much
i. mad, insane, angry
j. angry at, angry with, angry about
7. Have students rewrite each sentence using the correct expression.
   a. (Can, *May*) I go to the movies?
   b. The movie was (really, *very*) good.
   c. I (*think*, guess) she is not going to call me.
   d. Sally (just then, *then*) came into the room.
   e. I will meet you (*at*, at about) seven o'clock.
   f. I saw a (*tragic*, funny) accident in which three people were seriously hurt.
   g. That singer has (*much*, lots of) talent.
   h. The coach is (angry at, *angry with*) me.
   i. Losing the game has made me (mad, *angry*) enough to take extra practice.
   j. There are many things I do not enjoy about coming to school, such as getting up early, walking in the rain, being splashed by cars, waiting for class to begin (and etc., *etc.*).

Chapter 3: Putting Ideas Together in Sentences

An Overview of the Chapter

The opening portion of the chapter reviews the parts of speech and sentence parts, such as nouns, verbs, adverbs, conjunctions, determiners, and various forms of subjects, predicates, objects, and complements. It moves on to sentence patterns and covers, with supporting exercises, such patterns as negative, passive, imperative, exclamatory, and interrogative sentences. The chapter gives precise and explanatory information on the use and formation of the compound and complex sentence and stresses their value in the improvement of quality and proficiency in all student writing. Individual exercises are provided to encourage and enhance the student's ability in the combining of sentences to form more informative and effective sentence structures and patterns. The use of the phrase and clause is presented and explained. The chapter concludes with exercises and information designed to make students aware of fragmented and run-on sentences and to avoid their use.

Suggestions for Using the Chapter

Although the chapter appears in content and subject to be extremely academic, it often is helpful to apply the material to actual student-written work. One previously written composition, say at the beginning of the school year, could trigger the use of this chapter in an effort to improve the quality of what the student has already written. Oral reading of compositions and paragraphs, before and after rewrite, is a healthy activity in bringing personal and realistic motivations toward mastering the elements of the chapter. It is not always necessary to have the student read his or her own work, for hearing the work read by others often creates the desire for improvement. Care should be taken, however, to find strong points of quality in a student's work whenever and wherever possible. This recognition helps alleviate embarrassment and frustration.

The chapter has an ample number of exercises; however, some additional activities might be applied at the teacher's discretion.

1. At specified times after a writing assignment has been completed, extract specific weak and faulty sentences from student work and display these sentences using an overhead projector. Discussing, correcting, and revising the sentences in front of the class tends to cause students to be more aware of these errors when they write again. At times, students might correct the sentences on the overhead projector.

2. Have the class divide into two teams. Outline a sentence pattern on the board that the students are to copy in writing, forming a meaningful sentence. The first student to write a meaningful sentence, following that sentence pattern, raises his or her hand. The student reads the sentence to the class and, if correct, that student writes another pattern outline on the board. Continue until all students have had a chance to respond. If a student fails to complete a desired pattern, he or she is out of the game. The team with the most remaining members wins. The game could help relieve some of the tediousness often experienced in the learning of the various sentence patterns.

3. This is a parts of speech activity. Copy the following paragraph for duplication and give students the following directions.
   a. Identify the parts of speech of the ten underlined words in the paragraph. Place the name of that part of speech above the word.
   b. Rewrite the same paragraph using a different word, but the same part of speech, for each underlined word. Underline these words and circle each noun of a sentence which is the subject noun and each verb which is the predicate verb. Then find each prepositional phrase and draw an arrow from the preposition to its object.

   > It was early in the morning when Amos, the most <u>notorious</u> lobsterman on the point, <u>readied</u> his boat for the long day's gathering of traps and pulling of buoys. He <u>meticulously</u> checked to see if he had enough fresh bait to set <u>twenty</u> new traps with the tempting <u>morsels</u> for the ever-elusive lobster. If only his take were good today, he <u>thought</u>, as he started the engines and headed his boat out <u>past</u> the jetty <u>toward</u> the deeper waters and his family's trapping grounds. "The sea, <u>she</u> is so mysterious, dangerous, <u>yet</u> beautiful," he said aloud.

4. As a review test of their knowledge of parts of speech, ask students to complete the following. Other literary passages could be used to complete similar exercises in this or different aspects of writing.

1984 by George Orwell

It was a bright cold day in *April,* and the *clocks* were striking thirteen.
  1 2   3   4 5   6   7

Winston Smith, his chin *nuzzled* into his breast in an effort to escape the vile
    8   9   10

wind, slipped *quickly* through the glass doors of *Victory Mansions*, though not
           11   12

quickly enough to prevent a swirl of gritty dust from entering along with *him.*
 13   14

The hallway smelt of boiled cabbage and *old* rag mats. At one end of it a
                                     15

colored poster, too large for indoor display, had been tacked to the wall. It
depicted simply an enormous face, more than a meter wide: the face of a man
of about forty-five, with a heavy black mustache and ruggedly handsome
features. Winston made for the stairs. It was no use trying the lift. Even at
the best of times it was seldom working, and at present the electric current
was cut off during daylight hours. It was part of the economy drive in preparation for Hate Week. The flat was seven flights up, and Winston, *who* was
                                                           16

thirty-nine, and had a varicose ulcer above his *right* ankle, went slowly, rest-
                                          17

ing several times on the way. On each landing, opposite the lift shaft, the
poster with the enormous face *gazed* from the *wall.* It was one of those
 18   19   20

pictures which are so contrived that the eyes follow you about when you move.
BIG BROTHER IS WATCHING YOU, the caption beneath it ran.

a. Common Noun	e. Verb
b. Proper Noun	f. Adverb
c. Personal Pronoun	g. Adjective
d. Relative Pronoun	

1. *it:* _____	11. *quickly:* _____
2. *was:* _____	12. *Victory Mansions:* _____
3. *bright:* _____	13. *quickly:* _____
4. *cold:* _____	14. *him:* _____
5. *day:* _____	15. *old:* _____
6. *April:* _____	16. *who:* _____
7. *clocks:* _____	17. *right:* _____
8. *Winston Smith:* _____	18. *poster:* _____
9. *his:* _____	19. *gazed:* _____
10. *nuzzled:* _____	20. *wall:* _____

Chapter 4: Writing Better Paragraphs

An Overview of the Chapter

This chapter is designed to help students improve their ability to use those
paragraphing skills which apply particularly to the developmental or
"body" paragraphs of larger expository or argumentative essays.

A chart which identifies the most important characteristics of good paragraphing is provided for student reference and the main concepts of the chart are explained in the text. These concepts include *unity*, avoiding digression and closely developing one idea; *clarity*, presenting the main idea clearly and in clear relationship to the entire paragraph; *development*, using specific details, examples, reasons, steps, or comparisons to develop a main idea; and *coherence*, organizing a paragraph well and making effective use of transitions.

The chapter includes a great deal of practical advice about improving paragraph writing as well as many specific techniques and exercises aimed at increasing the ability of students to construct developmental paragraphs which effectively illustrate the concepts of unity, clarity, development, and coherence.

Paragraph length, techniques of transition within, between, and among paragraphs, developmental skills, and methods of organization are all treated in the chapter.

Finally, the chapter discusses writing paragraphs from personal knowledge and using specific information to write good paragraphs.

Suggestions for Using the Chapter

Since the focus of this chapter is on writing paragraphs as part of longer essays of exposition or argument, it would be helpful if students have some initial essay writing before beginning the chapter.

The chapter suggests that students choose three essays they have previously written in order to rate the developmental paragraphs of each and to discover those areas of paragraphing which they need to improve. A convenient rating chart is included on text page 71 for this purpose. It is then suggested that students review the chapter to improve their weaknesses in paragraphing.

Another way to begin the chapter is to have students write an essay of three or four paragraphs in length and to analyze that essay in terms of the criteria presented in the chart. If this second method is used, analysis by the teacher of several paragraphs using the overhead projector would be particularly helpful to students as a model for their own analysis. After this analysis students should individually study those sections of the chapter which treat their particular weaknesses, or the class may together review each section of the chapter.

A third way to begin the chapter is to choose one or two paragraphs which violate all of the criteria of good paragraphing. Using the overhead projector, these paragraphs could be analyzed with the class to point out apparent weaknesses. This analysis could be followed with a class review of the chapter.

These concepts of paragraphing are often very difficult for students to comprehend and master. For this reason, it is recommended that the teacher work closely with the class during the review of the chapter.

Since the paragraph is a basic unit of composition, the mastery of these skills will pay off whenever students are asked to write essays of several paragraphs. Along with the exercises included in the text, the following suggestions should prove helpful.

1. Have students carefully develop a paragraph of 75 to 100 words on the meaning or the importance or the need for one of the following topics:

money	taxes
faith	death
education	friendship
war	security
family	marriage

After they have carefully constructed and developed this paragraph and are satisfied that it is well written in terms of organization, clarity, unity, and coherence, have them scramble their final version by changing the order of their sentences. Ask students to

a. Turn in the scrambled versions to be mimeographed and given to the class the next day to be reordered. (If this is done, as each student's paragraph is reordered by the class, the student himself or herself could read the original aloud.) OR

b. Exchange their paragraph with one other student to attempt to unscramble the paragraph of the other and then compare the paragraph unscrambled with the original.

If the reordering comes close to the original, then the paragraph has probably been successfully written. If the reordering is impossible, then weaknesses in the paragraph should be discussed. Questions which might be asked are these:

Do sentences digress from the main idea or does every sentence in the paragraph belong?
Is there a single main idea in the paragraph?
What method or methods of development are used?
What method of organization is used?
What transitional devices are used?

2. Bring to class mimeographed magazine articles and discuss these in relation to the concepts of clarity, unity, coherence, and development.
3. Using a short story anthology or an essay anthology available to the class, have students discuss the characteristics of several opening paragraphs.
4. Using slides or still pictures, have students write a clear, coherent, unified, and well-developed paragraph on a topic suggested by the picture.

Chapter 5: Autobiography

An Overview of the Chapter

The chapter presents a step-by-step process by which a student can obtain information about himself or herself and organize this information in a permanent folder. Various methods of *searching* for information are presented. The element of *focus*, or purpose in gathering autobiographical information, is explained and suggested exercises in using the material are offered. The chapter concludes with exercises on *mapping* out, or arranging, the material gathered and selecting different *forms* of presentation, such as the news article, editorial, fable, poem, or resumé.

Suggestions for Using the Chapter

Due to the personalized nature of gathering, discovering, and developing information about oneself, it may prove useful if the teacher approaches this chapter in a less academic and more personal manner. Points of emphasis should be the students themselves, i.e., how much does each individual know about himself or herself? Is it important to know who, what, and why you are as you are? Students could be asked, *Do you know anyone more important to you than you*? This question often leads to interesting discussions and the teacher should use discretion on how to follow up or conduct the discussion. However, once the attitude for the chapter is established, motivation toward the accomplishment of the activities within the chapter tends to stand a better chance of being realized. Since this chapter and the activities are more individual-student oriented in terms of research and development, it may prove useful to introduce the chapter and then spend one lesson a week on the various sections as a standing out-of-class project or homework assignment.

1. In the final application of the skills and information developed during this chapter, students are asked to write a detailed autobiography. These might be mimeographed as a class booklet to be given to each student. It might be interesting for students to look at ten or twenty years later.
2. Have students write a series of memories that they might title, "It Always Happens to Me." These memories may have happened at many different times during their lives. The remembrances could become part of a life folder.
3. Have students write a series of memories that they might title, "The Happiest Moments of My Life." These memories may have happened at many different times. The remembrances could become part of a life folder.
4. If students don't do so already, have them try keeping a personal diary for two weeks. Tell them that they may keep this diary for themselves or may share it with you or their friends. Just keeping the diary, even if they do not share it, may give them some new insights into their own lives.

Chapter 6: Writing the Review of Nonfiction

An Overview of the Chapter

This chapter will help students to learn and develop the skills needed to write a thorough review of a work of nonfiction. The chapter includes many specific suggestions for approaching the review of nonfiction, and it is noted that many of these same suggestions may be applied to the review of any book.

Fiction and nonfiction are defined and methods of generating a successful and complete review of a nonfiction work are discussed in detail. Pre-reading activities are noted, along with specialized methods of reading for the purpose of reviewing. A set of criterion questions for evaluating nonfiction works is included, and suggestions are made for important activities to be completed after the book has been read but before the actual review has been written.

Finally, the chapter presents a process for the actual writing of the review. The process includes using notes that have been taken during the reading of the book in order to organize and compose a review which 1) *identifies* the book in a way that interests the reader and presents the reviewer's general opinion of the book, 2) *describes* the content of the book in some detail, 3) presents a personal *response* to the book which indicates and explains how the book affected the reviewer, and 4) *rates* or *evaluates* the work in a complete and thoroughly supported manner.

A very useful final evaluation chart is included on text page 120 to aid students in organizing their evaluation paragraphs. The book is judged as to whether it is reliable, informative, clear, interesting, well-written, and easy to use.

Sincerity and originality in book reviewing are discussed and a method for determining the quality of a book review itself is included (text page 125).

Suggestions for Using the Chapter

Since writing a detailed evaluative review of nonfiction will probably be new to most students in the class, it is strongly recommended that the class carefully work through the chapter together in preparation for the writing by each student of a major paper reviewing a significant work of nonfiction.

You may wish to assign the review to the class before beginning to teach the chapter. If this is done, the students will view the paper they must write as a goal or end product which they may continually work on while studying the chapter.

Working through the chapter and its exercises in order to learn the skills and methods of reviewing nonfiction will be challenging to students and everything the teacher can do to instill excitement into the process will be highly beneficial.

In addition to the exercises in the book, the following activities are suggested.

1. Explain to the school librarian the chapter project you are about to begin. Ask him or her to prepare a bibliography for the class which includes those works of nonfiction available in the school library. Recommend that the librarian bring the list to the class and discuss with them the variety of nonfiction works available. The purpose of

this discussion would be to stimulate interest in the reading of nonfiction.

2. Ask students to prepare a list of topics they would like to know more about. Mimeograph and distribute the list to the class for discussion. Find out during discussion if there are students in the class who have information about any of the topics listed. Ask students who have information to share it in an oral report to the class. The report should also include sources (including book titles) for the information presented.

3. Distribute to teachers in the building a list of topics compiled during exercise 2 and ask volunteers from the faculty to come to the class to discuss information about topics on the list with which they are familiar. Visiting teachers should also be prepared to recommend books on the topic which could be reviewed by students.

4. Complete exercise 3 using parents of class members instead of teachers.

5. Write each of the 40-50 topics on small pieces of paper and place the papers in a hat or box. Have students pick one paper from the hat or box and bring to class the next day the title of a book that has information about that topic.

6. Encourage students to choose a book for review that truly interests them. Once students have chosen the book and begun their own reviews, allow ten minutes at the end of each class period so that students in the process of writing their review will have the opportunity to ask necessary questions.

7. Mimeograph or prepare for the overhead projector several book reviews from newspapers or magazines and discuss the characteristics of several of these reviews.
   a. Do the reviews create reader interest?
   b. What techniques did the reviewer use to create this interest?
   c. Is the book *described* adequately?
   d. Is the reviewer's personal response to the book apparent?
   e. Is the judgment or evaluation of the book presented clearly and supported well?
   f. What transition words or sentences or paragraphs are used in the review?

Using the rating scale on text page 125, evaluate each of the reviews considered.

Chapter 7: Explaining Why

An Overview of the Chapter

This chapter develops a student's awareness and ability to analyze and reason through the use of logical steps. It fully explores such logic formulation as how to identify and separate cause from effect. Exercises are provided to enable students to become totally aware of the differences between the two. Errors in logical reasoning are pointed out and explained and exercises are given which enable students to identify such reasoning fallacies as *single cause fallacy, fallacy post hoc, fallacy of con-*

fusing cause with effect, and *fallacy of confusing association with causation.* The chapter concludes with lessons and exercises designed to aid in the student's creation and writing of a causal analysis essay. The lessons take the student through the logical sequence of introducing, developing, and concluding the essay. A self-evaluation and revision checklist for the essay of causal analysis is included so that students may complete an evaluation of their own essay.

Suggestions for Using the Chapter

By the very nature of the subjects and exercises in logic, cause and effect, and reasoning, many students will find in this chapter a new academic excitement and challenge. Although the overall purpose in studying the material is to have the students use these reasoning and logic skills to write a smooth essay of causal analysis, it will become apparent that the study can easily be connected to students' interests in a number of sciences and professions including law, psychology, sociology, physics, and others. This unique characteristic of the chapter allows the teacher to provide many supporting activities.

1. Have the students read one or more of the stories or plays below and complete the following activities:
   a. What is the major problem in each play or story?
   b. What character has this problem?
   c. What are the causes for the problem?
   d. What are the effects?

   Suggested Short Stories
   "The Rock Fight" by Robert Whitehill
   "The Lie" by Kurt Vonnegut
   "Paul's Case" by Willa Cather
   "Don't Ask Me to Deliver Anymore Death Messages" by William Saroyan
   (You should use any other short stories with which you are familiar.)

   Suggested One-Act Plays
   "The Valiant" by Hallworthy Hall
   "Pawns" by Percival Wilde
   "The Ring of General Macias" by Josefina Niggli
   "Sounds of Triumph" by William Inge
   "Before Breakfast" by Eugene O'Neill
   (You may select any other one-act plays with which you are familiar.)

2. Ask students to interview young children between the ages of two and five in order to determine the children's views on the causes of natural phenomena. When they interview the young child, students should be cautioned to accept any answer the child gives as correct and to encourage and praise the child as often as possible. Students could choose any of the following topics for their interview.

snow	rain	thunder	lightning
hail	clouds	leaves	rainbows
lakes	fog	rivers	oceans

One way of beginning the interview comfortably is to ask the child to draw a picture of whatever topic he or she will be interviewed on. The interviewer should bring crayons and paper to the child if pictures are to be drawn. After the picture is drawn, the child may be asked questions about the topic which stem from and relate to the picture that has been drawn. Interview questions should be directed toward determining what the child feels to be the cause of the natural phenomenon. Questions, such as "Where do leaves come from? How do leaves get their color?" will draw interesting answers from the child. The results of these interviews could be shared with the class for discussion. The exercise will give students insight into the reasoning process of young children and, consequently, into their own reasoning processes.

Chapter 8: The Essay of Persuasion

An Overview of the Chapter

This chapter introduces students to the basic elements and techniques of persuasive writing. Definitions are discussed and a continuum of persuasive types from reporting facts and expressing opinions to propagandizing and brainwashing are explored.

An overview which covers the important steps involved in the construction of a meaningful essay of persuasion is presented, and students are asked to consider topics for their own essay which will be developed during the chapter.

The steps students will work on in the process of writing their essay include deciding on a topic of persuasion, thinking through the details of a proposal for change, completing the necessary research needed for a convincing argument, identifying a particular audience, planning the essay of persuasion, and writing the essay.

The chapter suggests that students organize their persuasive essay around some improvement that they think should be made in a particular organization.

Methods of generating ideas, such as brainstorming a problem, conducting a systematic investigation of a problem, and using an instrument such as the "improvement suggester" which is provided in the chapter, are presented and questions of feasibility, acceptability, and effectiveness are raised.

Ways of working out details and identifying arguments are included with a special section on a variety of psychological appeals which will help students understand the psychology of persuasion more completely.

Audience selection and essay plans are explained along with methods of essay organization including writing the introductory paragraph, exploring the proposal, establishing convincing arguments, and concluding effectively.

A process for proofreading and evaluating the final copy of the persuasive essay is included.

Suggestions for Using the Chapter

This chapter on persuasion should be taught from beginning to end as a class unit of study. The chapter is tightly structured around the task of writing a persuasive essay. Throughout the chapter students are taught various techniques of writing a persuasive essay and are then asked to apply the techniques to the essay they are writing.

Completing the exercises provided in the chapter and keeping up with their own essay will be challenging for most students and teacher checkpoints, perhaps one or two a week depending on the class, are necessary if students are going to keep working on their writing as the chapter is studied. The best final essays should be read to the class and discussed.

Along with the activities of the chapter, the following might be helpful and interesting to students.

1. Ask students to identify two or three television advertisements which seem particularly successful. Then have the students describe the ads briefly and explain why the ads are successful.
   a. What is the purpose of the ad?
   b. How does the ad achieve its purpose?
   c. What techniques of persuasion are used in the ad?
2. Ask students to complete exercise 1 for a radio, newspaper, or magazine advertisement. These analyses of ads may be presented in written form or given to the class as an oral report.
3. Ask students to think of a topic and prepare an argument of persuasion to be given orally to the class. These could be written and presented individually or in pairs with each student in the pair taking the opposite side of the same issue. For example:

   Student A: There should be a structured discipline code at school.
   Student B: There should be a more lenient discipline code at school.

   If two sides of the same issue are presented, students in the class should evaluate the presentation in an effort to decide which student made the more convincing argument and why.
4. Have students think of some person that they dislike a great deal. Ask the students to develop a brief persuasive essay which convincingly explains to themselves why they should *not* dislike the person.
5. Ask students to think of a place, a person, a food, or an activity which they like very much. Have students write a persuasive essay to themselves which attempts to convince themselves that the place, person, food, or activity is *not* good.
6. Ask students to write a well-developed paragraph to persuade an audience that one of the following is true.
   a. A dependable car is hard to find.
   b. Television is educational.
   c. Smoking is hazardous to your health.
   d. Drinking alcoholic beverages is hazardous to your health.
   e. War is a necessary evil.
   f. The more books you read, the more intelligent you become.
   g. Firefighting is one of the most dangerous jobs in our society.

h. Football is a dangerous game.
i. Summer is the best time of year.
j. Education is very important.
7. Ask students to create a TV ad for a *new* product. Students should create an interesting name for the product and write at least one paragraph which could serve as the narration for a TV advertisement. Then students might create a story board for their ad following this format.

VANISHING BOTTLES AND CANS

Picture	Picture	Picture

Narration: At last an incredible technical advance to eliminate pollution caused by bottles and cans.

Yes, a NEW can that disappears after emptied of its contents.

. . . . .

Picture	Picture	Picture

Narration: . . . .

Chapter 9: Writing in Other School Subjects

An Overview of the Chapter

This short chapter emphasizes the importance of two kinds of school writing—library papers and essay answers—in all subject areas, only one of which is English. The chapter begins by outlining the features of the library paper and discusses the following: locating sources, taking notes, writing the rough draft and documenting, and preparing the final draft. A self-evaluation and revision checklist is provided for students to judge their work. Taking essay tests is a skill which students will want to master. The chapter provides tips on planning, writing, and proofreading answers for most effective use of test time. A chart provides definitions for key words often encountered in essay questions.

Suggestions for Using the Chapter

The chapter presents a good opportunity to emphasize the applicability of writing skills to all other subject areas. Students sometimes tend to compartmentalize learning so that skills do not transfer. Motivation for this work should not be a problem once students understand that writing skills acquired will cross over to other areas and improve their effectiveness in other school subjects. To augment the exercises provided in the text, the following might be useful.

1. If possible, arrange with a colleague in social studies or science to work on cooperative assignments for a library paper in their subject area. You would be responsible for English form and effectiveness, while your colleague would judge the paper on content correctness.
2. Have students bring in essay questions they have encountered in tests. The class might evaluate the clarity of the questions and outline possible responses to them.

Chapter 10: Writing Effective Letters

An Overview of the Chapter

The form and process of writing effective letters is the focus of this chapter. The six parts of a formal business letter are presented and discussed with models and exercises provided. Developing effective content within the form of a business letter is presented, with content being divided into three sections of concentration: identification, detailed statement of purpose, polite statement of conclusion. The chapter focuses specifically on the proper and effective method of writing formal letters to public officials. Tone, appearance, and organization are centers of concentration with exercises provided to reinforce these aspects of form, style, and technique. Instruction on how to compose the proper social note concludes the chapter. Models and exercises are provided to aid in the understanding of the information presented in this section.

Suggestions for Using the Chapter

Since the writing of letters is a very real and practical activity, it is important that this chapter not be passed over lightly. Once the skills of writing an effective letter are realized, there is often a lessening of student frustration caused by their desire, but inability, to express information, ideas, feelings, and opinions to personal as well as public figures. The chapter can most effectively be used after Chapters 1 through 9 have been studied. Using this chapter in its proper sequence allows the teacher to utilize and reinforce material and concepts already covered. Activities such as the following may be a useful addition.

1. Have students write a letter to a public official attempting to persuade the official to support a belief that they hold strongly.
   a. Perhaps a specific lake, river, or stream is polluted or not being taken care of properly and you want something done about it.
   b. Perhaps there is not enough work for young people in the summer and you would like something done to improve the situation.
   c. Perhaps there is no section at professional athletic events priced low enough for young people to attend and you would like something done.

There are many ideas students can arrive at that require a letter of persuasion. Encourage them to think about possibilities.

2. Ask students to think back to Chapter 6 and their nonfiction book review. Then have them complete the following:

   a. Write a letter to the publisher of the book requesting information on how to contact the author of the book.

   b. When this information is obtained, write a letter to the author requesting additional information about some aspect of the book that you have reviewed.

   c. If an answer is forthcoming, write a letter of appreciation.

3. Have students write a letter to the local town or city newspaper expressing their views on the causes and effects of a problem in their school or community. Refer to Chapter 7 when beginning this activity.

4. Have students write a letter to a well-known person whom they truly admire, thanking him or her for the way that he or she has enriched their life or asking him or her questions about their art, profession, or life.

5. Explore the interest in establishing a pen-pal relationship with a student in a foreign country. If your class is interested, find out how to begin the process. The school librarian may be helpful. There are several educational agencies which may be of help to you in getting started with this endeavor.

Chapter 11: Reviewing and Revising

An Overview of the Chapter

The chapter takes the students through the sequential steps in the evaluation, proofreading, and revision process: evaluating the composition as a *whole*; checking the *paragraphs* for interest, development, structure, function, and revision; checking *sentences* for punctuation, structure, form, and possible revision and improvement; checking *words* for spelling, usage, choice, punctuation, and possible revision. Exercises are provided in both proofreading and revision. Commonly used correction symbols are presented with explanations.

Suggestions for Using the Chapter

This short, but vital, chapter should be taught prior to teaching Chapters 5 through 9. Once the chapter has been taught, students should refer to it whenever a writing assignment is required. The chapter provides abundant exercise material for sharpening skills and developing a conscious awareness of the importance of proofreading and revision.

Proofreading and Revision

In particular, punctuation marks improve or distort both the clarity and euphony of writing. Because of this, students should learn to proofread and correct their errors in punctuation.

Teachers have traditionally used an explanation and drill approach to teach punctuation skills. While this approach remains an effective one, it does not guarantee success nor does it provide much activity for students.

One suggestion which might help the class is to have a small group of students (perhaps for extra credit) fill in a chart similar to the one shown below. The chart could then be mimeographed and given to each student as a proofreading reference sheet for his or her notebook. The same or another group could make a large poster version of the chart for classroom display.

PUNCTUATION CHART			
Name	Symbol	Definition of Use	Example
colon	:	Mark used after the salutation of a business letter, after a word introducing an explanation, example, series, or quotation.	1. Dear Mr. Day: 2. The following are the most important ingredients: salt, pepper, oregano, and thyme.

Spelling and Revision

Throughout the year, have students keep a list of all words misspelled in their compositions. They should keep the list of words in a separate section of their notebooks. For each word they should note whether the error was corrected in a proofreading stage of composing or whether it was not corrected until the teacher returned the paper.

This process will help students become more aware of their spelling errors and any patterns of spelling error which occur in their writing. It will also provide them with a list of commonly misspelled words.

Chapter 12: A Writer's Handbook

An Overview of the Chapter

As the introduction to the chapter notes, it contains three types of information arranged alphabetically: grammatical terms and definitions, usage notes, and writing tips.

Suggestions for Using the Chapter

There are probably two helpful ways the chapter can be used. Most teachers will probably wish to use it as a reference handbook, referring to it in class when common problems develop and requiring students to use it in checking individual mistakes. Some teachers, on the other hand, may wish to teach a few items in order each week as a kind of "first-thing-Monday" activity, thus covering the entire handbook by the end of the school year.

EVALUATING WRITING

A successful composition program requires three types of evaluation: *diagnostic*, *formative*, and *summative*. While the development of reliable and valid measures that will yield scholarly research findings requires the consultation of expert psychometricians, it is possible for the classroom teacher to use less complex measures and processes for all three types of evaluation which will provide general measures of both individual and school progress.

Diagnostic Measurements

At the beginning of the year it is recommended that two types of diagnostic measures be used. The first, and less important in our view, is an objective test of knowledge and information about the elements of writing. On pages 41-47 the teacher will find two such tests, one of which can be used at the start and the other at the end of the year. Each of these tests includes items measuring five types of knowledge: *word usage, sentence form, composition terminology, sentence parts,* and *revision problems.* This objective test samples all the important knowledge objectives of this text. The results of the diagnostic test can help the teacher make a general assessment of the class's background and can pinpoint individual deficiencies.

A more valid measure of writing ability, of course, is the student's own writing. Here we have provided three diagnostic writing assignments which the teacher can administer early in the year. They are designed to measure the student's ability to write in three of the modes emphasized in the text: expressive, persuasive, and referential. These three assignments should be given during the first few weeks of school so that the teacher is able to have for each student a valid measure of writing ability before formal instruction begins. The assignments should be made so that the student has ample time for conception, incubation, production, and revision; but the teacher must assure, of course, that the writing represents the student's own work.

The care with which these three pieces are analyzed and the use made of the results will depend upon the teacher's and the school system's need for reliable data—and the amount of technical help available to the teacher. Teachers and school systems interested in rigorous and comprehensive evaluation programs might wish to consult two excellent sources:

Cooper, Charles. "Measuring Growth in Writing," *The English Journal*, 64 (March 1975), 111-120.
Diederich, Paul. *Measuring Growth in English*. Urbana, IL: National Council of Teachers of English, 1974.

Teachers who wish to use less formal diagnostic approaches can use their individual judgment in assessing the results of the objective test and the writing samples, dividing the class into three groups:

Group 1: Those students who demonstrate they already possess the skills taught in this text.

Group 2: Those students ready to use the text who do not possess the skills taught in it.

Group 3: Those students so seriously deficient that they do not seem ready to use this text.

Students in Group 1 will profit from the use of Book 4 in this series; they can also assist the students in Group 3, who will require individualized remediation.

In making these diagnostic assessments, most teachers will probably wish to use a holistic grading process. In holistic grading the teacher reads the paper and makes a general assessment of its overall quality, rather than rating individual aspects of the essay. While holistic grading has been found to be a highly reliable and useful way of making general assessments, it does not give the student or the teacher specific information about competencies and deficiencies. Readers wishing a more detailed analysis of the strengths and weaknesses of holistic grading can turn to John Mellon's excellent monograph, *National Assessment and the Teaching of English* (Urbana, IL: National Council of the Teachers of English, 1975).

Regardless of the method of grading used, however, these three papers should be kept in the cumulative writing folder described below, to be used as part of the summative evaluation.

Formative Evaluation

Formative evaluations, given throughout the year, are the assessments made of student writing on a continuing and ongoing basis. While the type and frequency of such formative evaluation will vary with the teacher (influenced by such factors as size of class, student needs, and school district policy), an analysis of the research on grading suggests that a process like the following might prove to be both feasible and productive.

1. Students keep their own cumulative writing folder. A standard third-cut manila file folder can be used for this purpose. The student keeps all important writing in the folder as well as the Cumulative Writing Record, which the student maintains on an ongoing basis. An illustration of the Cumulative Writing Record is shown on page 39.
2. For each major writing assignment the teacher identifies the important traits expected in a successful response to the assignment. Ordinarily no more than five such traits should be identified for each assignment, so that the student focuses efforts on important objectives. These traits are of course derived from the

nature of the assignment. Suggestions for the traits identified for particular assignments can be found both in the text itself and in the set of duplicating masters available with this series. These traits become the criteria by which the writing is evaluated; they are the basis of an evaluation form developed by the teacher which the students can use as the cover page of their essay. A sample evaluation form is shown on page 40. This method of evaluating essays is called a "primary trait" process, and according to some assessment specialists seems to yield more useful results than holistic grading.

3. On the day on which a major writing assignment is due, the teacher organizes the class into an "evaluation workshop." The students are given fifteen minutes to revise and evaluate their own work, marking the evaluation form in ink. Each student then pairs up with another student for peer evaluation, which probably requires another fifteen minutes, depending on the length of the paper. The student reader reports his or her judgment on the same evaluation form, using pencil. The last part of the period is used for expressive writing, free reading, or individualized instruction.

4. While the evaluation workshop is being conducted, the teacher holds five-minute evaluation conferences with students on a scheduled basis. The conference is used to review previous work, to evaluate the present assignment, and to help the student with individual difficulties.

5. The teacher reads all papers submitted, recording his or her evaluations in colored pencil or ink. The student thus is able to see at once the results of self-, peer-, and teacher-evaluation.

The teacher makes it clear to the class that, while all papers will be read carefully, some may not be graded and many will not be annotated extensively. One reasonable solution to the paper-load problem, in fact, is for the teacher to systematize the kinds of reading given a paper. Thus a teacher who assigns four major papers in a given nine-week period for each student would read one paper in conference, annotate one paper with much care, make a general response to one paper, and let one paper go ungraded. The teacher may wish to give students the right to indicate a preference here, with the understanding that one out of every four papers will receive extensive annotation. The sample evaluation form on page 40 provides space for the students to check one of the following statements:

_____ Prefer a grade only on this; no comments necessary.
_____ Prefer a grade with written criticism.
_____ Prefer written comments only.
_____ Prefer individual conference and grade.
_____ Prefer no grade on this paper.

The system thus provides ongoing feedback from multiple sources without requiring the teacher to spend an excessive amount of time in grading papers.

Summative Evaluation

Summative evaluation, in our use of the term, refers to the end-of-year evaluation which assesses overall growth in writing when compared with the base-line data yielded by the diagnostic measures. As noted above, two types of summative instruments are provided: an alternate form of the objective test which can be used as a post-measure; and three essay assignments which can be used to assess growth in writing.

As previously explained, teachers and districts interested in rigorous program evaluations should refer to the Cooper and Diederich pieces for useful suggestions. In the absence of such rigorous school-wide evaluations, individual teachers can still use the pre- and post-measures to assess for the student and themselves the extent of growth in writing. Each student should be asked to review the test scores on the objective tests and the two sets of evaluative themes, responding in writing to these questions:

1. How do I assess my overall progress in writing?
2. In what specific ways has my writing improved most?
3. In what specific ways has it shown least improvement?
4. How do I wish my writing to improve next year?

These written self-evaluations can then be used in an end-of-year conference between student and teacher.

CUMULATIVE WRITING RECORD						
School Year _____ School _____						
Student's Name _____ English Class _____ English Teacher _____						
Date Writing Assignment Due	Date Submitted	Title	Type	Grade	Major Strengths	Major Weaknesses

EVALUATION FORM

School _____

English Teacher _____ English Class _____

Student's Name _____

Title of Writing Assignment _____

Date Due _____   Date Submitted _____

Intended Audience _____

Main Purpose _____

Criteria for this assignment   *Evaluation*

	5 Poor	4 Fair	3 Good	2 Very good	1 Excellent
1. Uses language appropriate to audience.	5	4	3	2	1
Comments _____					
2. Persuades audience with honest and effective methods.	5	4	3	2	1
Comments _____					
3. Organizes essay so as to interest audience and move to action.	5	4	3	2	1
Comments _____					
4. Shows correct form in usage, punctuation, and spelling.	5	4	3	2	1
Comments _____					
5. Uses mature sentence style.	5	4	3	2	1
Comments _____					
Overall Evaluation	5	4	3	2	1

Grading Preferences

_____ Grade only   _____ Conference, grade

_____ Grade with comments   _____ No grade

_____ Written comment only

Student Reader _____

OBJECTIVE TEST: FORM A

I. Knowledge of Terms. Listed below are ten terms used in discussing writing. For each term you will find four possible definitions. Write the letter in front of the correct definition as your answer.

1. POINT OF VIEW
   a. The sentence that contains the main idea of an essay
   b. The literal or dictionary definition of a word or term
   c. The physical or mental angle from which a story is told
   d. A visual device which provides negative transition
2. CONNOTATION
   a. An inappropriate level of language
   b. The literal or dictionary definition of a word
   c. Objective words with little emotional impact
   d. The emotional meaning or tone of a word
3. PERSONIFICATION
   a. A figure of speech in which inanimate objects are given human qualities
   b. The concluding paragraph of an autobiographical essay
   c. A personal account or diary
   d. The main idea in an introductory paragraph
4. METAPHOR
   a. The concluding sentence of a formal letter
   b. A literary comparison of two unlike objects or things
   c. An essay of four paragraphs or more
   d. A comparison of unlike objects or things using the words **like** or **as**
5. SIMILE
   a. A comparison of unlike objects or things using the words **like** or **as**
   b. A humorous essay of persuasion
   c. A literary comparison of two unlike objects or things
   d. A figure of speech that makes an obvious exaggeration
6. UNITY
   a. The major section of a formal outline
   b. Another name for the topic sentence of a paragraph
   c. A quality of a paragraph in which all sentences relate to one idea
   d. Using comparisons to develop an argument
7. COHERENCE
   a. A paragraph lacking a central idea
   b. A paragraph quality based on organization and transition
   c. Expressing two points of view in a single paragraph
   d. A poetic ability to create imagery

8. BIBLIOGRAPHY
   a. Writing that is immature and childish
   b. A note at the bottom of a page indicating the source of a quotation
   c. The study of biblical writing
   d. A list of the sources used in writing a paper
9. CAUSAL ANALYSIS
   a. A pattern of organization in which events are told in their order of importance
   b. A formally written resumé
   c. Essay writing which identifies problems of cause and effect
   d. A casually written personal note
10. DEVELOPMENT
   a. The use of complex sentences to improve the tone of an essay
   b. A way of using verbal or visual devices to bias the audience
   c. A writing skill which clearly expands and completes the main idea
   d. A method of proofreading written composition

II. Sentence Sense and Types of Sentences. Read each item below carefully. Decide which term best defines the type of expression. Use the letter beside each term for your answer.

a. Compound sentence   f. A sentence in the
b. Complex sentence   passive voice
c. Compound-complex   g. Run-on sentence
   sentence   h. Sentence fragment
d. Imperative sentence   i. Interrogative sentence
e. Negative sentence   j. Appositive

11. Billy, my cousin from Indiana, is coming to visit me.
12. This is not going to take me very long.
13. The truck was driven by a woman wearing an army uniform.
14. We went on vacation, and we drove through the hills of New Hampshire for two hours before finding a motel.
15. Jon bought a foreign sports car and he is very proud of it.
16. Go get your raincoat.
17. After the thunderstorm, he went fishing for trout.
18. The Red Sox are playing the Yankees I hope the game isn't rained out.
19. Will you ever give me back my pencil?
20. After I finish all of this homework.

III. Sentence Parts. In the sentences below, identify each sentence part in bold type. Use the letters beside the listed sentence parts for your answer.

a. Simple Subject   d. Indirect Object
b. Simple Predicate   e. Predicate Nominative
c. Direct Object   f. Predicate Adjective

g. Clause
h. Phrase

i. Compound Predicate
j. Compound Subject

During the summer, my **Aunt Claudia and Uncle Al** took a
21   22

trip around the world. They **drove** to New York **and flew**
23   24   24

to London. Later, Aunt **Claudia sent me** a letter from
25   26 27

Istanbul. In the note she said that Istanbul was **beautiful**.
28

After they left Istanbul, they traveled by plane to Hong Kong
29

where Uncle Al became **leader** of a tour group.
30

IV. Sentence Patterns.
Below are listed some basic sentence patterns. Read the sentences which follow the list and correctly identify the pattern of each. Use the letters for your answer.

a. Subject + Predicate
b. Subject + Predicate + Direct Object
c. Subject + Predicate + Indirect Object + Direct Object
d. Subject + Predicate + Predicate Nominative
e. Subject + Predicate + Predicate Adjective
f. Subject + Predicate + Adverb

31. Chin saw his relatives.
32. The team was late.
33. Carlo became captain.
34. Susan is beautiful.
35. My sister gave me a ticket to the dance.

V. Word Choice.
Each of the sentences below contains one of the errors in the following list. Identify the error in each sentence. Use the letters beside the list of possible errors as your answer.

a. The sentence makes poor use of repetition.
b. The sentence uses words of negative connotation.
c. The sentence contains too many general words.
d. The sentence uses examples of slang expressions.
e. The sentence uses improper sensory words.
f. The sentence uses no concrete nouns.
g. The sentence uses an incorrect word.
h. The sentence uses words of positive connotation.

36. The very nice person was good to me.
37. My cousin is fat.

38. The lines of time on the elderly man's face gave him character.
39. The big man went into the big store to buy a big box of cookies.
40. The screaming bell rang with a loud buzz.
41. After the tornado everything was alright in our house.
42. It was a super party but it was crumby of his mother to make the guys wear ties.
43. She wrote her letters on elegant stationary.
44. He ran down the street and ran around the corner and quickly ran up the stairs to his house.
45. Democracy guarantees liberty, justice, and freedom.

VI. Revision and Proofreading. Each of the five sentences below needs revision in one of the following areas. Use the letters beside the choices for your answers.

    a. The sentences should be combined into one sentence.
    b. A word is needed.
    c. An error in pronoun reference needs to be corrected.
    d. Punctuation is needed.
    e. Rearrangement needs to be corrected.

46. The lake was surrounded by towering trees. They were birches and pines.
47. A small boat could be seen in the distance a single person was seated in it.
48. The little dog ran to its and licked his face.
49. The children all ran to the bus so he wouldn't be late for school.
50. The committee of senators in room 208 are meeting.

OBJECTIVE TEST: FORM B

I. Knowledge of Terms. Listed below are five terms used in discussing writing. For each term you will find four possible definitions. Write the letter in front of the correct definition as your answer.

1. DENOTATION
    a. The proper use of concrete nouns
    b. The literal or dictionary definition of a word
    c. The correct use of cause and effect in developing an argument
    d. The emotional meaning or tone of a word
2. ECONOMY
    a. The use of abstract words to suggest meaning
    b. The combining of a concluding and introductory paragraph in a final composition
    c. The most important aspect of a writer's style
    d. Eliminating all words that are unnecessary to the meaning of a sentence or paragraph
3. TRANSITION
    a. Words, phrases, or sentences which contribute to the smooth flow of ideas from one paragraph to the next
    b. Words which begin every topic sentence
    c. The main sentence in a developmental paragraph
    d. The details and examples used to support the main ideas of an essay
4. FIGURE OF SPEECH
    a. A narrative or descriptive essay
    b. A factual account of an event
    c. A poetic expression used to create an image
    d. A type of poem
5. ORGANIZATION
    a. The use of research material to write an analytical essay
    b. A systematic plan of development used to obtain coherence
    c. The use of comparison and contrast to prove a point
    d. The use of varied sentence structures and patterns

II. Sentence Sense and Types of Sentences. Read each item below. Carefully decide which term best defines the type of expression. Use the letter beside each term for your answer.

a. A compound sentence	g. A run-on sentence
b. A complex sentence	h. A sentence fragment
c. A compound-complex sentence	i. An interrogative sentence
	j. An appositive
d. An imperative sentence	k. A compound negative passive interrogative sentence
e. A negative sentence	
f. A sentence in the passive voice	l. An exclamatory sentence

6. The truck was not driven by a boy, was it?

7. I am not going to the movies.
8. It's getting very late I'll miss the opening kickoff.
9. The kickoff was not seen by me or you.
10. Shut the door.
11. The car was driven by a famous rock star.
12. They were rewarded with prizes after winning the race.
13. I want to go on vacation, and I want to take my brother with me because he needs a rest.
14. Although everyone came to the party last night.
15. Did she ever call you?
16. I don't like answering questions on this test; they are too difficult for me.
17. My tropical fish, a Montezuma guppy, is very rare.
18. Thank God, it's Friday!
19. Down the street where the tree fell.
20. The yachtsman was painting his boat, a beautiful 40-foot cabin cruiser, when the fire broke out.

III. Sentence Parts. In the sentences below identify each sentence part in bold type. Use the letters beside the listed sentence parts for your answer.

a. Simple Subject
b. Simple Predicate
c. Direct Object
d. Indirect Object
e. Predicate Nominative
f. Predicate Adjective

g. Adverbial Clause or Phrase
h. Prepositional Phrase
i. Adjective Clause or Phrase
j. Compound Predicate
k. Compound Subject
l. Object of a Preposition

Last night I dreamt that **you and I** went on a cruise
  21   22   23   24

to the **West Indies**. We **listened and danced** to the music of
    25   26

a **steel band**. The music was **loud** and rhythmic. The leader
  27   28

of the band gave **me** a **chance** to play one of the drums. The
         29   30

band leader had been a **chief** of an island tribe and knew the
        31

costumes of the native West Indian peoples perfectly.
Before I awoke, the boat **which we sailed on** slowly
                    32

disappeared in the mist.

IV. Sentence Patterns. On the next page are listed some basic sentence patterns. Read the sentences which follow this list and correctly identify the pattern. Use the letter beside each pattern for your answer.

a. Subject + Predicate
b. Subject + Predicate + Direct Object
c. Subject + Predicate + Indirect Object + Direct Object
d. Subject + Predicate + Predicate Adjective
e. Subject + Predicate + Predicate Nominative
f. Subject + Predicate + Adverb

33. All motorcycle drivers wear helmets.
34. The bass are running.
35. Louise is a cheerleader.
36. Brigitta is gorgeous.
37. We were last.

V. Word Choice. Identify each word in bold type in the following sentences. Use the letter beside the list of word types for your answer.

a. Repetition
b. Concrete noun
c. Abstract noun
d. General word
e. Specific word
f. Slang expression
g. Jargon
h. Word of negative connotation
i. Word of positive connotation
j. Sensory word
k. Incorrect word

38. The **buzzing** of a mosquito always annoys me.
39. The old man **hobbled** down the dirt path using his gnarled hickory stick for support.
40. The **slender** young woman hoped to be a fashion model.
41. The manager of the baseball team knew the **squeezeplay** was on.
42. The old wooden **shack** at the top of the mountain burned down.
43. The boy happily **excepted** the prize money.
44. It was really a **super** dance.
45. His **fear** of height kept him from driving across bridges.

VI. Revision and Proofreading. Each of the five sentences below needs revision in one of the listed areas. Match the sentence with the needed revision.

a. The sentences should be combined.
b. A word is needed.
c. An error in pronoun reference needs to be corrected.
d. Punctuation is needed.
e. Verb agreement needs to be corrected.

46. I throw the ball at him but he did not catch it.
47. Sally and Jim and one of the Capalleti twins is going to the party.
48. I haven't seen the movie **Citizen Kane**. It is a film classic. It stars Orson Welles.
49. My uncle the one you saw yesterday, used to be a movie extra.
50. The leaders of the protesting nuclear energy group were taken to jail yesterday by two police officers. He was told that he would stay overnight.

ANSWERS TO OBJECTIVE TEST: Form A

1. c	11. j	21. h	31. b	41. g
2. d	12. e	22. j	32. f	42. d
3. a	13. f	23. c	33. d	43. g
4. b	14. c	24. i	34. e	44. a
5. a	15. a	25. a	35. c	45. f
6. c	16. d	26. b	36. c	46. a
7. b	17. b	27. d	37. b	47. d
8. d	18. g	28. f	38. h	48. b
9. c	19. i	29. g	39. a	49. c
10. c	20. h	30. e	40. e	50. e

ANSWERS TO OBJECTIVE TEST: Form B

1. b	11. f	21. g	31. e	41. g
2. d	12. b	22. a	32. i	42. b
3. a	13. c	23. b	33. b	43. k
4. c	14. h	24. k	34. a	44. f
5. b	15. i	25. h, i	35. e	45. c
6. k	16. a, e	26. j	36. d	46. e
7. e	17. j	27. l	37. f	47. e
8. g	18. l	28. f	38. j	48. a
9. e, f	19. h	29. d	39. e	49. d
10. d	20. j, b	30. c	40. i	50. c

Diagnostic Assignment #1

Think back over your school experiences to the most memorable teacher you have ever encountered. This teacher could be from your earliest years in school or from the present. Describe your memory of the teacher as though you were writing in a diary or a personal journal. Include in your description why this teacher is special or outstanding in your memory.

Diagnostic Assignment #2

Assume that a well-educated, eccentric millionaire is sponsoring a contest in your town. There is only one prize—a million dollars. In order to win, contestants must write a detailed letter which convinces the millionaire that they should be the one to receive the prize. Enter the contest by writing your letter which attempts to persuade the millionaire to choose you!

Diagnostic Assignment #3

You have been assigned to work with an exchange student from a foreign country. Your first responsibility is to write an article to be published in "The Foreign Exchange Newsletter" which will be mailed to all exchange students. Your article must present an interesting explanation of a typical day at your school. Write the article.

Summative Assignment #1

Think of all the members of your family including grandparents, aunts, uncles, cousins, and so forth. Choose the most unusual, imaginative, colorful, and unique individual from among your family members. This person may be living or deceased. Describe the family member as though you were writing in a diary or personal journal. Include in your description all of the details that contribute to the qualities that make this particular relative so memorable to you.

Summative Assignment #2

Suppose that you are attempting to get elected to an important position on the student council of your school. If you achieve the position, you will have an opportunity to make many decisions about the school and how it is run. As part of your campaign effort, write a detailed explanation to be published in the school newspaper as to why you are the best candidate to represent the student body.

Summative Assignment #3

Assume that you have been asked to explain to a child between the ages of three and five one of the following topics: how to tie shoes, how to scramble eggs, how to ride a bicycle, how to use a skateboard, how to swim, how to catch a fish. Write an interesting and detailed explanation about one of the topics. Remember your audience.

ANSWERS TO TEXT EXERCISES

Where an exercise has only one correct answer, that answer is given below. When an exercise calls for a short individual response, a sample response is given in parentheses. Answers are not given for open-ended writing exercises since responses will vary so much.

CHAPTER 1

PAGE 6: (top)
(Everything is relative.)
(We live in a very difficult age.)
(To be full, life needs both joy and suffering.)
(Mistakes of judgment are permissible when reason is free to challenge them.)
(People will blame their faults on anything but themselves.)

(bottom)
(Corn on the Cob:

Sight	Sound	Touch	Smell	Taste
yellow	crunch	slippery	fresh	sweet
hilly	smack	hot		steamy buttery)

PAGE 12: (top)
a. (The steps of the stairs are like the struggles of my life.)
(The vacuum cleaner picks up pieces the way writing uncovers thoughts.)
(My life came to a stop sign where everything good came to a halt.)
(My writing pushed into the corners of the world.)
b. (My mind is a peanut butter jar, opened by learning.)
(I turn the handle of new ideas to get the lid off my opinions.)
(I force my mind into the grip of study.)
(It takes knowledge to turn the handle of prejudice and get my mind open.)

(bottom)
Rhythm to "I've Been Working on the Railroad":
(I've been studying my homework
Day after day.
I've been studying my homework
And my hair is getting gray.
I still hear the teacher asking,
"Are your lessons done?"
I can hear myself replying,
"Every single one!")

PAGE 16: Exercise 1
(It all happened when I went downtown for my mother. She wanted a package mailed at the main post office. I caught the bus down. The fifty-one took me within seven blocks. I walked the seven blocks and waited in line. It got late and dark. The bus never came. I started walking home but I fell down.)

Exercise 2
E, B, F, A, C, G, D

PAGE 18:
1. (toiling like an ant)
2. (before anything drastic happens)
3. (insecure as an inchworm dangling in the wind)
4. (lifeless as a stack of lumber)
5. (tense as a clockspring)
6. (rested like a fog on the sea)
7. (noble as a knight)
8. (the quiet hours before dawn)
9. (precious)
10. (light-hearted as a young girl)

PAGE 19:
(Now came the hard years. In those days in the country, school was held three months in summer and three in winter. Little girls did not go to school much in winter, since it was cold and not many of them had warm clothing. Therefore, my school days were limited.

Although I was kept busy helping at home and with the neighbors, I left home when I was twelve years of age to earn my own living as what was then called a hired girl. This was a grand education for me in cooking and housekeeping and in moralizing and mingling with the outside world.

I went to live with a family by the name of Mrs. and Mr. Thomas Whiteside. They were lovely people and well along in years. I was cared for by them as if I were a child of their own. They were Presbyterians by creed. One of my duties was to drive the horse "Old Black Joe" to church for them on Sunday mornings. I would place bouquets on the pulpit in the church and was taught always to remember the text.

I lived with the Whitesides for three years, earning for Mrs. Whiteside, who was an invalid who died while I was there.)

CHAPTER 2

PAGE 21:
1. T-F
2. T-F
3. T
4. T
5. F
6. T-F
7. T

PAGE 23: Exercise 1
a. The students pretended to be interested, but they were really bored.
b. Effective
c. The trees swayed in the cool September wind, bending gently in the breeze.
d. Effective
e. Wood is an economical fuel. But it can also be dangerous, since green wood can cause chimney fires.

PAGE 25: Exercise 1
Hearing: clash, chug, hiss, whine
Taste: biting
Sight: rotary
Touch: stinging
Smell: (Passage does not contain a sensory word appealing to sense of smell.)

PAGE 27: Exercise 1
fear jumped at him: personification
like a great animal: simile
wind moaned: personification
rose into a sudden howl: personification
horror seized him: personification
like a nightmare made real: simile

PAGE 28:
howling of the wind: personification
Feeling came hurtling against him: personification
it flung him cowering away: metaphor/personification

PAGE 30: Exercise 1
a. (It's an interesting book.)
b. (She is a kind person.)
c. (The man stumbled down the street.)
d. ("Stop," he shouted.)

PAGE 33: Exercise 2
a. accept
b. adapt
c. among
d. conscience
e. capitol

CHAPTER 3

PAGE 39: Exercise 1
a. S + be + PA
b. S + LV + PN
c. S + Vt + DO
d. S + Vi
e. S + LV + PA
f. S + be + PA
g. S + be + ADV
h. S + P + IO + DO

PAGE 41: Exercise 1
a. Cars should not go faster than 55 miles an hour.
b. My parents cannot dance very well.
c. Checkers is not an exciting game.
d. Oil cannot be found in rocks.
e. People will not land on the planet Mars.

Exercise 2
a. Does Jill sit next to you in music class?
b. Is green my favorite color?
c. Did we stay up until after midnight?
d. Can you buy posters at the school store?
e. Is New York the largest city in the United States?

Exercise 4
a. How good it was to see you!
b. What a good time we had at the picnic!
c. Your pizza is awful!

PAGE 44: Exercise 1
a. (Although the advertisements were colorful, the cautious consumers read them with care.)
b. (One brave sailor was the only survivor of the great disaster.)

PAGE 50: Exercise 1

a. (Tom and his friend ate pizza and drank milkshakes.)

b. (Sally put on and laced her sneakers and ran from the bench onto the field.)

PAGE 51:

c. (The campers and their guide hiked through the woods to the lake.)

d. (René doesn't like art or music; however, she likes gym.)

PAGE 52: Exercise 1

a. (Although the weather was cold, he went for a walk.)

b. (Because photography is a rewarding profession, I will learn to use a camera.)

c. (I was very interested while the speaker told about colonial life.)

d. (When Mr. Jones speaks, many people fall asleep.)

e. (I will not start the game until you get here.)

Exercise 2

a. (Because they crave excitement, people find daily routines boring.)

b. (After he finished high school, my brother joined the army.)

c. (The problem seemed easy compared to the others I had solved.)

d. (If you wish to be a teacher, a sense of humor is essential.)

e. (Dinner will be ready after the program is over.)

PAGE 53: Exercise 3

a. (Because we didn't have any homework, we went to the movies.)

b. (Beth was happy because she got a perfect score.)

c. (Jogging, which is a popular sport, is good for your health.)

d. (As the gentle breeze blew, the boat glided across the lake.)

e. (Inflation is a serious problem that influences jobs.)

PAGE 54: Exercise 1

a. (The man who lives near me is moving tomorrow.)

b. (After they had eaten, they went to the game.)

c. (Since we saw you, we came over to talk.)

d. (The dress which Sally bought was expensive.)

e. (Whenever we go there, we'll let you know.)

f. (The top was all that we could see.)

g. (The teacher who went with us was nervous.)

h. (Although he saw it before, he didn't recognize it.)

PAGE 55: Exercise 2

a. (I believed what I saw.)

b. (The money we have is not enough.)

c. (She told me that her aunt was ill.)

d. (The store did not have what I wanted.)

PAGE 56:

a. (After the rain came, the game stopped but the fans remained in their seats.)

b. (Since you asked the question, I'll give you the answer, but don't tell anyone else.)

c. (After Dan completed the training program, he went to work at the main office and his family was proud of him.)

d. (Though I worked hard at my small garden, it was worth the effort, and the snow peas were delicious.)

PAGE 57: Exercise 1

a. (Jim, the center, is the tallest player on the team.)

b. (I gave my mother roses, her favorite flower.)

c. (I saw *Star Wars*, my favorite movie, three times.)

Exercise 2

a. (Farm products, corn and wheat, are essential to our country.)

b. (I'd love to visit Mexico, the sunny land to our south.)

c. (Microwave ovens, the homemaker's dream, have become popular during the past ten years.)

PAGE 58:

(Some two million Americans are now enrolled in prepaid legal plans. These plans are similar to medical group insurance plans; they offer a full range of legal services including divorces, wills, house closings, and even counsel for criminal offenses. The employer and the employee both contribute a small amount, about one dollar a week. The employee can then get free legal services any time he or she needs a lawyer. Some people are afraid that these plans can cause problems. Attorneys might use the plans to encourage people to get legal help who really don't need it. Legal costs could also sky-rocket, just as medical costs have increased with medical insurance. Those people who disagree believe that prepaid legal services will help middle-class families stay out of legal trouble. These legal plans will allow middle-class families to obtain the aid of a lawyer before it is too late. At any rate the plans are definitely here to stay.)

PAGE 62: Exercise 1
(As a result of the plantation system, Southern white women often did little manual work and were generally not responsible for the care of their own children.)

Exercise 2
(Bought as a child by a Boston woman, Phyllis Wheatley was educated by her owner and became a well-known poet.)

Exercise 3
(Since slaves were considered property, not human beings, they had no personal or civil rights.)

PAGE 63: Exercise 1
(Baseball is a popular sport that is played and watched by millions of people every year.)

Exercise 2
(Baseball has a very interesting history.)

Exercise 3
(Immigrants from England introduced a game called "rounders," which later became baseball, to America.)

PAGE 65: Application 1
c. (What a powerful storm a tornado is!)
d. (The parade was watched by thousands of people.)
e. (Herb was frightened by the sight.)
f. (Is pollution a serious international concern?)

PAGE 66: Application 1
a. (I watched the expert surfers riding the big waves that crashed onto the beach.)

b. (The Anasazi, a Navajo tribe now known as Pueblos, lived in the desert hundreds of years ago and built cities before Columbus discovered America.)

PAGE 67:
c. (Amelia Earhart, the first woman to fly the Atlantic Ocean alone, won honors for the flight by setting a new speed record.)

Application 2
(As Mike walked along the mountain trail on this warm and sunny day, he could hear trucks on the highway about a mile away. Mike stopped to rest. Suddenly, he heard a loud sound coming from the trees behind him. Mike jumped, turned around, and saw something strange.)

CHAPTER 4

PAGE 71: Exercise 2
Original article:
(Spider is a small, eight-legged animal that spins silk. Spiders are best known for the silk webs they spin. They use their webs to catch insects for food. Even insects that are larger and stronger than spiders cannot escape from the threads of a spider's web.

All spiders spin silk, but some kinds of spiders do not make webs. The bolas spider, for example, spins a single line of silk with a drop of sticky silk at the end. When an insect flies near, this spider swings the line at it and traps the insect in the sticky ball.

All spiders have fangs, and most kinds of spiders have poison glands. A spider's bite can kill insects and other small animals, but few kinds of spiders are harmful to man. In North America, only six kinds of spiders have bites that can harm man. These spiders are the brown recluse spider, the sack spider, the black widow, the brown widow, the red-legged widow, and the varied widow. Of the four "widow" spiders, only the females are known to bite man. Many persons are afraid of spiders. But only hurt or frightened spiders bite human beings.

Spiders are helpful to man because they eat harmful insects. Spiders eat grasshoppers and locusts, which destroy man's crops, and flies and mosquitoes, which carry diseases. Some large spiders eat such animals as mice, birds, lizards, frogs, and fish. Spiders even eat each other. Most female spiders are larger and stronger than male spiders, and often eat the males.

Spiders live anywhere they can find food. They can be seen in fields, woods, swamps, caves, and deserts. One kind of spider spends most of its life under water. Another kind lives near the top of Mount Everest, the world's highest mountain. Some spiders live in houses, barns, or other buildings. Others live on the outside of buildings—on walls, on window screens, or in the corners of doors and windows.

There are more than 29,000 known kinds of spiders, but scientists believe there may be as many as 50,000 kinds. Some kinds are smaller than the head of a pin. Others are as large as a man's hand. One spider, a South American tarantula, measured 10 inches (25 centimeters) long with its legs extended.

Many persons think spiders are insects. But scientists classify spiders as *arachnids*, which differ from insects in many ways. Spiders have eight legs. Ants, bees, beetles, and other insects have six legs. Most insects have wings and *antennae* (feelers), but spiders do not. Other arachnids include daddy longlegs, scorpions, and mites and ticks.

Spiders may be short and fat, long and thin, round, oblong, or flat. Their legs are short and stubby, or long and thin. Most spiders are brown, gray, or black. But some are as beautifully colored as the loveliest butterflies. Many of these spiders are so small that their colors can be seen only with a microscope.

A spider has no bones. Its tough skin serves as a protective outer skeleton. Hairs, humps, and *spines* (bristles of skin) cover the bodies of most spiders.

A spider's body has two main sections: (1) the *cephalothorax*, which consists of the head joined to the *thorax* (chest); and (2) the *abdomen*. Each of these sections has *appendages* (attached parts). A thin waist called the *pedicel* connects the cephalothorax and the abdomen.)

PAGE 81:
(Chimps are probably the closest kin to humans in the animal world. A chimp named Washoe in Oklahoma has learned more than 100 sign-language gestures he can use to communicate with his trainer. Washoe has communicated with these gestures since the 1960s. A female chimp named Lana, who communicates on a computer console, has learned to communicate in a system called Yerkish. Yerkish is a system of geometric symbols that stand for English words. Two chimps named Sherman and Austin have even been trained to communicate with each other.)

CHAPTER 5

PAGE 86:
 b. (Where were you born?)
 c. (What relationship does Helen Jones have to you?) (Who is Helen Jones?)
 d. (What large city have you ever lived in?) (Where have you lived?)
 e. (What caused your family to scatter?)

CHAPTER 6

PAGE 104: Exercise 2
 a. 300-399
 b. 600-699
 c. 100-199
 d. 900-909
 e. 920-929

Exercise 3
 Public Speaking 450: Language
 Anatomy of a Cat 572: Science
 Raising Farm Cattle 620: Technology
 Understanding Yourself 150: Psychology
 World Book 010: Encyclopedia
 The Life of Gertrude Stein 921: Biography
 Eating Your Way Through Greece 917: Travel
 Rembrandt's Great Works 752: Arts
 Appreciation of Poetry 822: Literature
 Plato 172: Philosophy
 Basic Algebra 520: Science
 World Trade 370: Social sciences

PAGE 109: Exercise 1
 a. 1960s
 b. Reference to Stockholm
 c. Mainly scientific, but some popular. See reference to *Science* magazine.
 d. Trust

PAGE 110: Exercise 2
a. pages 87-8
b. Circadian rhythms
c. 6
d. 46-7, 53-4, 55-57, 87
e. good

PAGE 115: Exercise 3
a. (Although a specific topic sentence is not included, the paragraph clearly identifies the structure of the book and explains the concept of each of the book's three sections. More detail could be included but basically, the paragraph is fine.)
b. (The paragraph lacks detailed development. Not enough detail is given to develop the topic sentence.)
c. (This is very poorly written. The three sentences of the paragraph could be combined into one. The "theory" of the author which should be the topic sentence is not clearly stated.)

CHAPTER 7

PAGE 128: Exercise 1
Event
a. Bicycle accident
b. Business partner locked another partner in a freezer.
Cause
a. Dogs knocked rider from bike.
b. Business partner A forgot business partner B was in the freezer when he locked it for the night.
Effect
a. Rider fractured bone in elbow.
b. Business partner B received a bad case of frostbite.

Exercise 2
a. (His car will be repossessed.)

PAGE 129:
b.
I. (Public will want explanation from the mayor.)
(Mayor will attempt to explain to the public.)
(Backers will threaten to drop their support.)
II. (Will not be reelected and will possibly be punished.)
(Will be praised for its honesty and ability.)
III. (Attempt to identify and get apologies from those responsible for the slander . . . possible punishment.)
(Would be considered irresponsible and possibly lose support and circulation.)
(Would support the mayor.)

PAGE 130: Exercise 4
a. (Tripped.)
(Lost her balance.)
(Was pushed.)
b. (Applied for it and passed qualifying test.)
(Was the fastest mile runner in the state.)
(Was the only applicant to fulfill a specific quota necessary under the rules of the scholarship.)
c. (Bribed her teachers.)
(Was very intelligent.)
(Was of average intelligence but studied very hard and was prepared for all the examinations.)
d. (He had not paid many outstanding traffic tickets.)
(He was mistaken for a bank robber.)
(He was found landing his airplane on the highway and this was against the law.)
e. (His car would not start and it was his only way to get to work.)
(The subway on which he was riding broke down.)
(His alarm clock did not wake him and he slept late.)

PAGE 131: Exercise 5
a. (She was made to stay in her playpen.)
(Her brother was spanked.)
(She broke her arm.)
b. (He has more time to study, doesn't have to work.)
(He is on the university track team and competing for the Olympics.)
(He can now study to become a doctor.)
c. (She was identified as being dishonest and suspended from school along with the teachers.)
(She was awarded the scholastic trophy.)
(She developed self-confidence and went on to college.)
d. (He was fined $2000.)
(He was found to be not guilty and was paid damages.)
(His pilot's license was taken from him.)
e. (He was made to stay one hour longer the next day.)

He was taken out to dinner by his kind secretary.)

(He bought a new alarm clock.)

PAGE 132: Exercise 1

a. Truck driver ignored a flashing warning signal.

b. 9 cars derailed, 37 people killed, 95 injured.

PAGE 133: Exercise 2

a. (A special mystique surrounds Ted Williams that causes him to remain famous.)

b. (The statement that he has remained "larger-than-life" and that time cannot diminish this quality indicates the essay will explain more.)

c. (Handsome, six batting championships, 521 home runs, last of the .400 hitters, veteran of 19 years of baseball, .634 slugging percentage second only to Babe Ruth, his way of doing things which brought feuds with press.)

d. Paragraph 5

e. (They admire his self-confidence and his results.)

f. (Allows the reader to know that Williams is still alive and what he is doing now. Expands the idea that he is larger-than-life and has a certain mystique surrounding him. Yes.)

g. (Paragraphs 4-8 provide details which explain the continual popularity of Ted Williams. Paragraph 3 is a transition paragraph.)

h. (Yes, it does seem to conclude, though a restatement of the mystique and charisma of Ted Williams would provide a more satisfactory conclusion.)

PAGE 139: Exercise 2

a. Weak plan: tends to have the single cause fallacy. More causes should be mentioned, if not fully illustrated. *Introduction* and *Conclusion* should not be part of outline.

b. Satisfactory

CHAPTER 8

PAGE 146: Exercise 1

a. O	c. O
b. R	d. PE

Exercise 2

a. F	c. FO
b. O	d. F

PAGE 147:

e. FO

Exercise 3

a. (The writer is trying to get the reader to buy a heating pad from the Appliance Center-All Stores.)

b. (The writer is trying to get the reader to accept the idea that television advertising directed at children is very harmful in that it gives children an appetite for sugar and makes them nag their parents.)

CHAPTER 11

PAGE 199: Exercise 3

There is no clear pattern of organization. It lacks unity. Word choice is poor and the paragraph is poorly developed.

(*Rewrite:* There are many good reasons to become a class officer. You can, through your efforts, improve conditions in school life; moreover, you can develop important leadership skills which will be useful to you long after you have completed your schooling. Lastly, this experience will add an important ingredient to your college application.)

Exercise 4

No topic sentence. Two examples are provided for an idea that has not been stated.

(*Rewrite:* Teenage crime is becoming a problem in our community. Car theft is one example of the problem we all face. Another example is vandalism, especially in school buildings.)

Exercise 5

a. (The Indian scout crept silently through the underbrush; no one heard him.)

(No one heard the Indian scout as he crept silently through the underbrush.)

b. (Everyone liked to watch Elvira dance because she was an expert dancer.)

(Elvira was an expert dancer; therefore, everyone liked to watch her dance.)

c. (It was hot in the morning and in the afternoon; however, it was cool in the evening.)

(Although it was hot in the morning and in the afternoon, it was cool in the evening.)

Exercise 6
(Dear Mr. McCleary,
Your speech was excellent. We were very interested in what you had to say. No one has ever explained developments in the space program to us as clearly and effectively as you did. Your talk was a great success. Thank you very much.
Sincerely,)

Exercise 7
a. polished
b. gurgle
c. clanged
d. embarrassed
e. ferociously

NOTES

NOTES

NOTES